Everyday Mathematics®

Skills Link™

Cumulative Practice Sets

PENNSYLVANIA DEPARTMENT OF EDUCATION
Act 195 / 90 Year 1999-2000

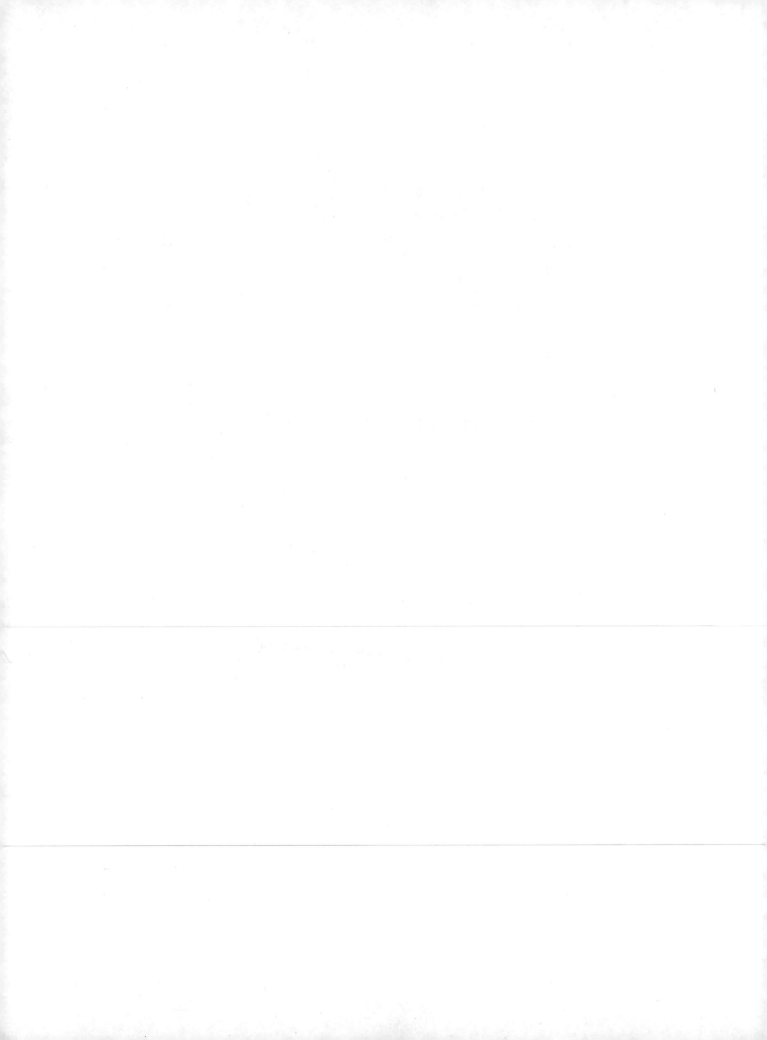

Everyday Mathematics®

Skills Link™

Cumulative Practice Sets

EVERYDAY LEARNING®

Chicago, Illinois

ISBN 1-57039-737-6

2 3 4 5 6 7 8 9 CU 02 01 00 99

Contents

Practice Set 1

1. Write each number.

2. Draw a 1 picture.

3. Draw a 2 picture.

4. How many cars?

_____

- - - - - - - -

_____

5. How many rabbits?

_____

- - - - - - - -

_____

Use with or after Unit 1.

Practice Set 2

1. Write each number.

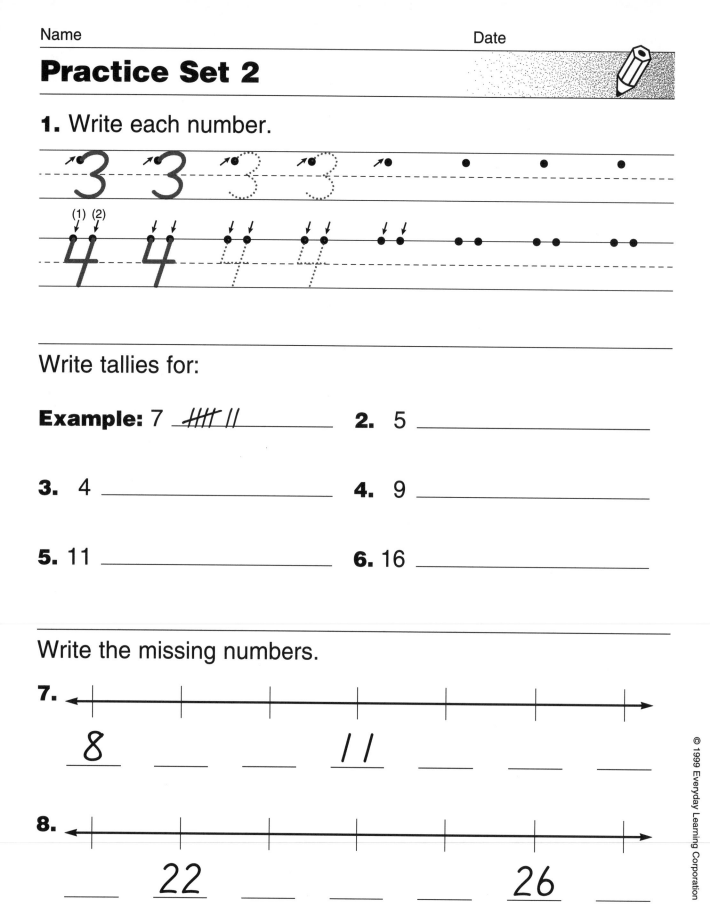

Write tallies for:

Example: 7 ⫻⫻ //

2. 5 _____

3. 4 _____

4. 9 _____

5. 11 _____

6. 16 _____

Write the missing numbers.

7. 8 ___ ___ 11 ___ ___

8. ___ 22 ___ ___ ___ 26 ___

Practice Set 3

How much money?

1.  _____ ¢

2. 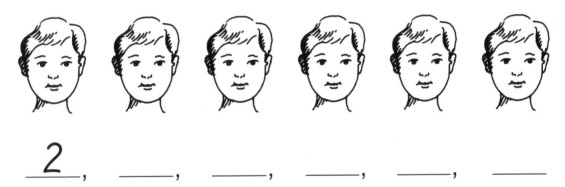 _____ ¢   **3.** _____ ¢

---

4. How many eyes? Count by 2s.

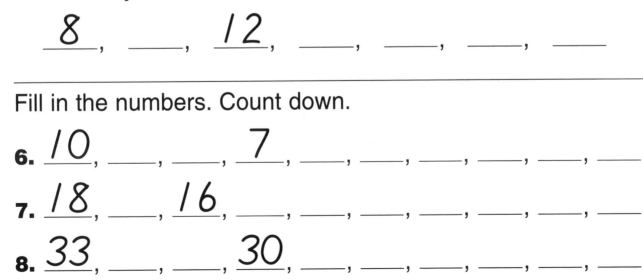

_2_, _____, _____, _____, _____, _____

5. Count by 2s.

_8_, _____, _12_, _____, _____, _____, _____

Fill in the numbers. Count down.

6. _10_, _____, _____, _7_, _____, _____, _____, _____, _____

7. _18_, _____, _16_, _____, _____, _____, _____, _____, _____

8. _33_, _____, _____, _30_, _____, _____, _____, _____, _____

Use with or after Unit 1.

Practice Set 4

1. How many fingers? Count by 5s.

_5_ , _10_ , _____ , _____ , _____ , _____

2. Count by 5s.

_40_ , _____ , _____ , _55_ , _____ , _____ , _____ _____ , _____

Count each group of tally marks.

Write the number.

Example: ＨＨＴ ＨＨＴ /// _13_

3. ＨＨＴ /// _____

4. ＨＨＴ ＨＨＴ ＨＨＴ / _____

5. ＨＨＴ ＨＨＴ / _____

6. ＨＨＴ ＨＨＴ ＨＨＴ ＨＨＴ _____

---

7. Write each number.

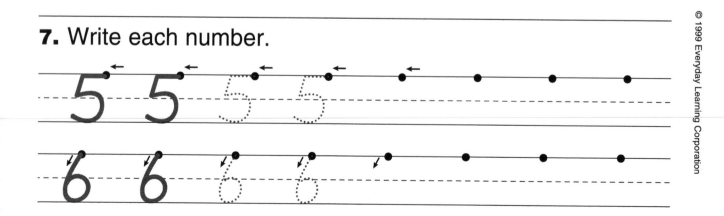

Practice Set 5

What's My Rule?

1. in ↓

Rule

1 more

out ↓

in	out
2	3
3	4
4	
5	
6	

2. in ↓

Rule

1 less

out ↓

in	out
7	6
8	
9	
10	
11	

3. Write each number.

7 7 7 7 7

8 8 8 8 8

Write the missing numbers.

4. 34 ___ ___ 37 ___ ___ ___

5. 51 ___ 53 ___ ___ ___

Use with or after Unit 1.

Practice Set 6

1. How many toes? Count by 10s.

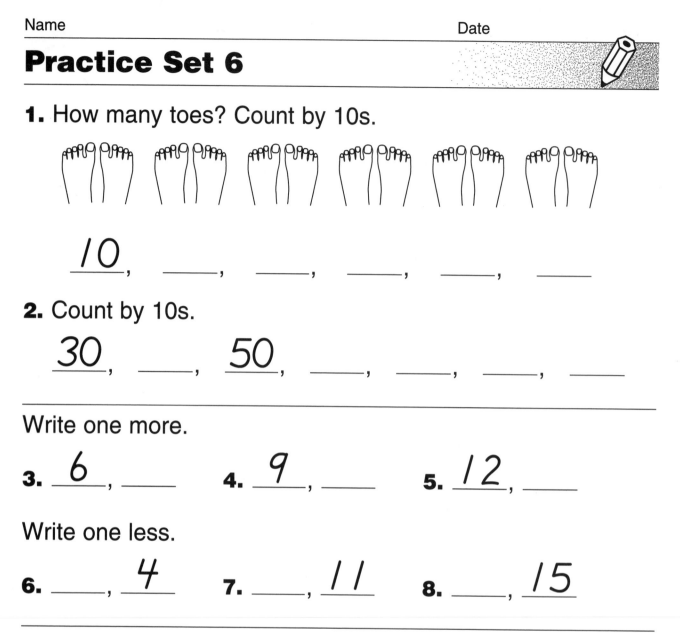

__10__, _____, _____, _____, _____, _____

2. Count by 10s.

__30__, _____, __50__, _____, _____, _____, _____

Write one more.

3. __6__, _____   **4.** __9__, _____   **5.** __12__, _____

Write one less.

6. _____, __4__   **7.** _____, __11__   **8.** _____, __15__

Complete each number family.

Example:

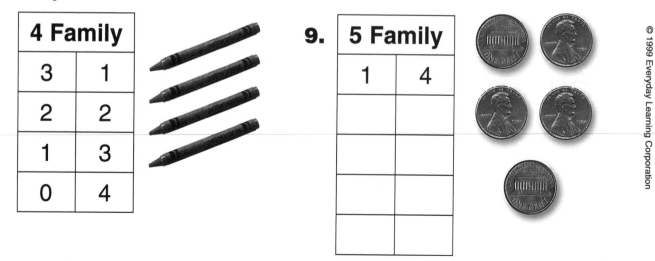

4 Family	
3	1
2	2
1	3
0	4

9.

5 Family	
1	4

Practice Set 7

1. Write each number.

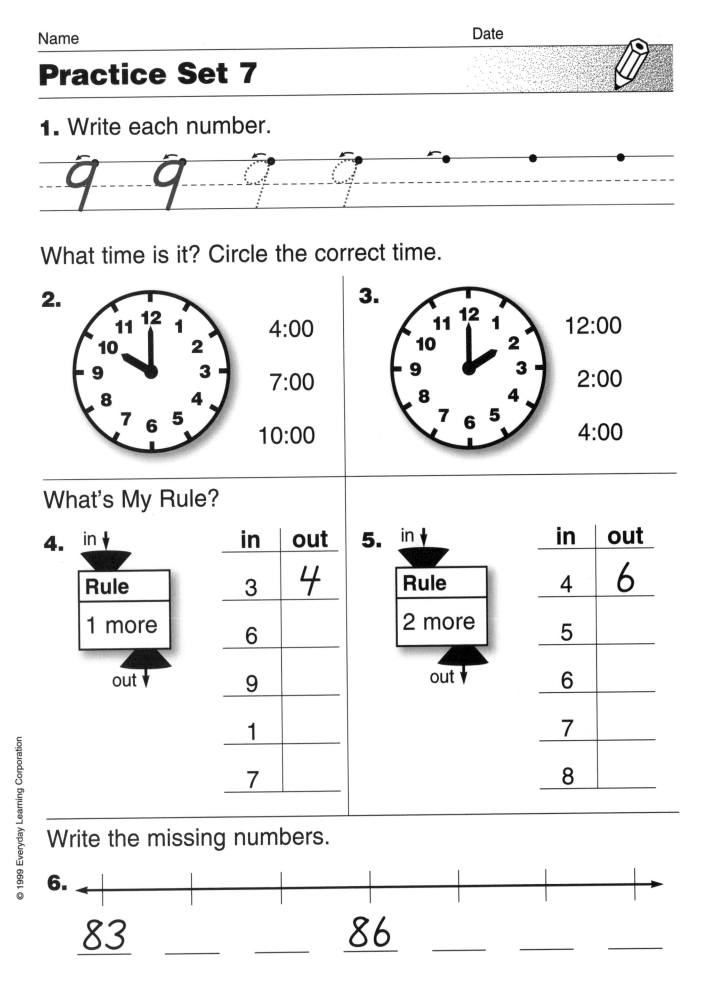

What time is it? Circle the correct time.

2.

4:00

7:00

10:00

3.

12:00

2:00

4:00

What's My Rule?

4.

in ↓

Rule

1 more

out ↓

in	out
3	4
6	
9	
1	
7	

5.

in ↓

Rule

2 more

out ↓

in	out
4	6
5	
6	
7	
8	

Write the missing numbers.

6.

83 ___ ___ 86 ___ ___ ___

Use with or after Unit 1.

Practice Set 8

Fill in the missing numbers. Count down.

1. _27_, ___, _25_, ___, ___, ___, ___, ___, ___, _18_

2. _39_, ___, ___, _36_, ___, ___, ___, ___, ___, ___

3. _50_, ___, ___, _47_, ___, ___, ___, ___, ___, _41_

How much money?

4. _____ ¢ or $._____

5. _____ ¢ or $._____

6. _____ ¢ or $._____

Use the tally chart. Answer each question.

Number of People in My Family	
2	///
3	⊥⊥⊥⊥
4	⊥⊥⊥⊥ ⊥⊥⊥⊥ ⊥⊥⊥⊥ /
5	⊥⊥⊥⊥ ⊥⊥⊥⊥ //
6	//
7 or more	

Answer each question.

How many children have

7. 5 people in their family?

_____ children

8. 4 people in their family?

_____ children

9. 2 or 3 people in their family?

_____ children

Use with or after Unit 2.

Practice Set 9

1. Begin at 25. Connect the dots.

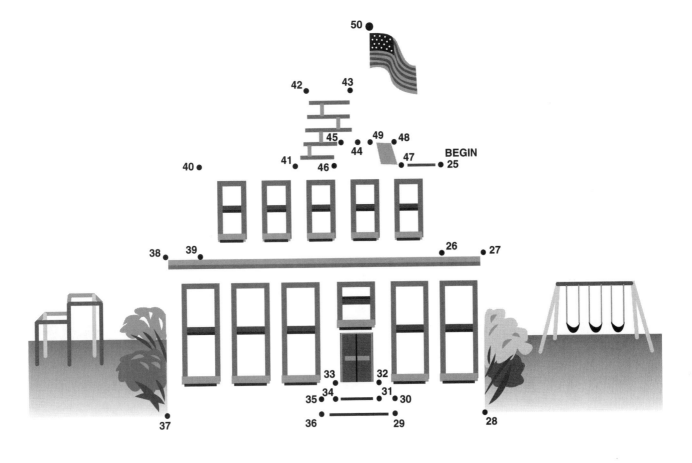

Record the time.

2.

about _____:00

about _____ o'clock

3.

about _____:00

about _____ o'clock

Use with or after Unit 2.

Practice Set 10

Write the numbers before and after.

1. ____, *17*, ____   **2.** ____, *30*, ____   **3.** ____, *39*, ____

4. Write the number.

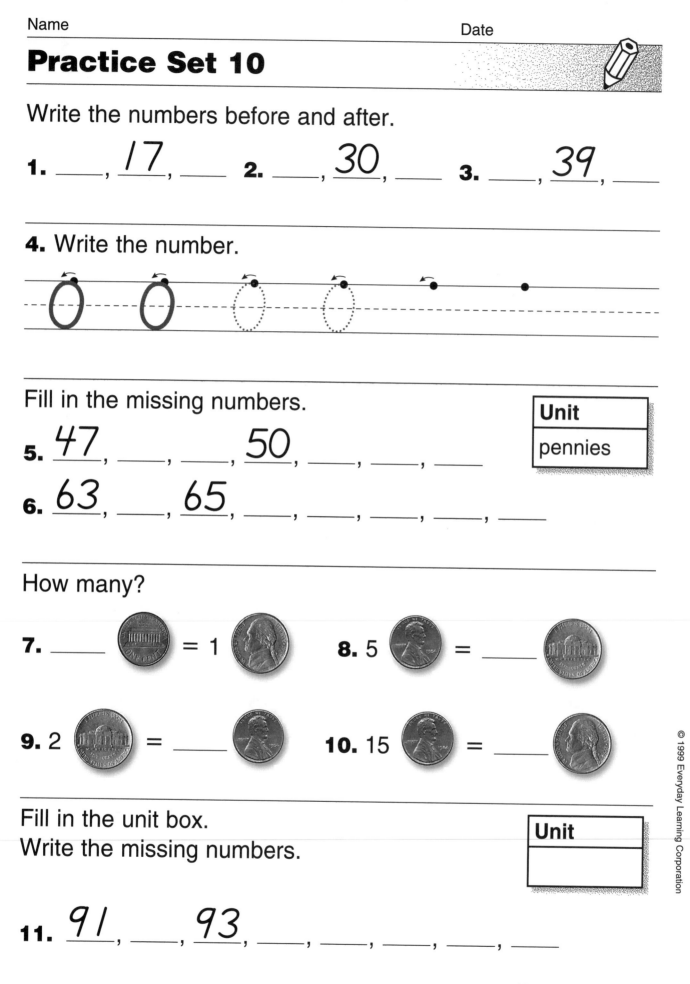

Fill in the missing numbers.

Unit
pennies

5. *47*, ____, ____, *50*, ____, ____, ____

6. *63*, ____, *65*, ____, ____, ____, ____, ____

How many?

7. ____ 🪙 = 1 🪙   **8.** 5 🪙 = ____ 🪙

9. 2 🪙 = ____ 🪙   **10.** 15 🪙 = ____ 🪙

Fill in the unit box.
Write the missing numbers.

Unit

11. *91*, ____, *93*, ____, ____, ____, ____, ____

Use with or after Unit 2.

Practice Set 11

1. Fill in the missing numbers on the calendar.

			October			
Sunday	Monday	Tuesday	Wednesday	Thursday	Friday	Saturday
		1	2			5
6	7			10	11	12
	14			17		
20			23		25	
	28			31		

Show the total. Draw Ⓝ and Ⓟ.

2.

	Total
	$.09 or 9¢

3.

	Total
	$.17 or 17¢

Use with or after Unit 2.

Practice Set 12

What's My Rule?

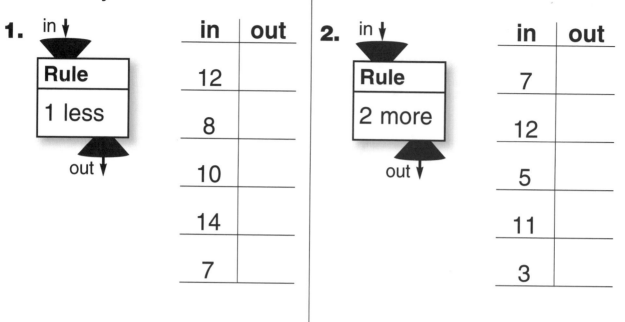

1.
in ↓

Rule
1 less

out ↓

in	out
12	
8	
10	
14	
7	

2.
in ↓

Rule
2 more

out ↓

in	out
7	
12	
5	
11	
3	

Record the time.

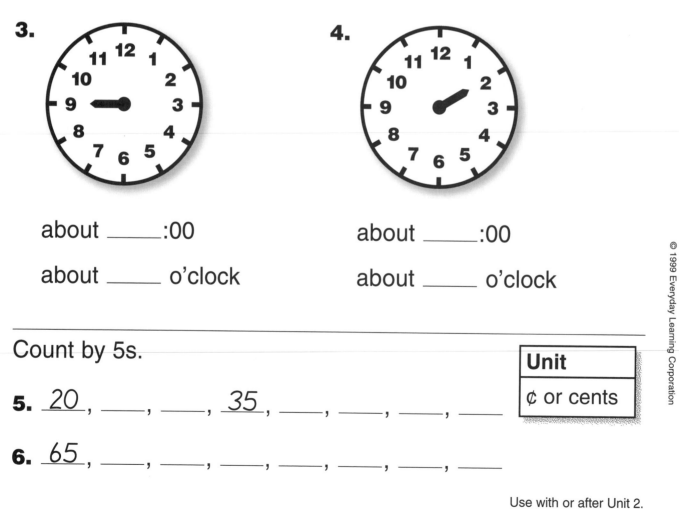

3.

about _____:00

about _____ o'clock

4.

about _____:00

about _____ o'clock

Count by 5s.

Unit
¢ or cents

5. _20_, ____, ____, _35_, ____, ____, ____, ____

6. _65_, ____, ____, ____, ____, ____, ____, ____

© 1999 Everyday Learning Corporation

Use with or after Unit 2.

Practice Set 13

How much money?

1. _____ ¢ or $. _____

2. _____ ¢ or $. _____

3. _____ ¢ or $. _____

Complete each number family.

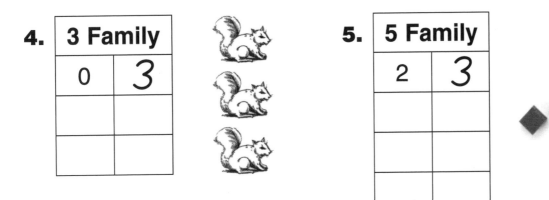

4.

3 Family	
0	3

5.

5 Family	
2	3

Write the numbers before and after.

	before	number	after
Example:	13	14	15
6.		20	
7.		36	

	before	number	after
8.		41	
9.		29	
10.		47	

Practice Set 14

Count by 10s.

Unit
¢ or cents

1. _10_, ____, _30_, ____, ____, ____, ____, ____

2. _40_, ____, ____, _70_, ____, ____, _100_, ____

Show the total. Draw (D), (N), and (P).

3. [ ]   Total
$.22 or 22¢

4. [ ]   Total
$.18 or 18¢

5. [ ]   Total
$.26 or 26¢

Write a total. Then draw (D), (N), and (P) to show your total.

6. [ ]   Total
$.____ or ____¢

Practice Set 15

How many?

1. 1 (dime) = _____ (penny)

2. 20 (penny) = _____ (dime)

3. 2 (nickel) = _____ (dime)

4. 2 (dime) = _____ (nickel)

Write the missing numbers.

5.

83 ___ ___ 86 ___ ___ ___

6.

102 ___ 104 ___ ___ ___ ___

Write tallies for each number.

7. 14 _____   **8.** 17 _____

9. 20 _____   **10.** 23 _____

Count each group of tally marks.
Write the number.

11. ⊬⊬ /// _____   **12.** ⊬⊬ ⊬⊬ /// _____

13. ⊬⊬ ⊬⊬ ⊬⊬ _____   **14.** ⊬⊬ ⊬⊬ ⊬⊬ ⊬⊬ / _____

Use with or after Unit 3.

Practice Set 16

Fill in the unit box.
Count by 2s.

1. _10_ , _12_ , _14_ , ___ , ___ , ___ , ___ , ___ , _26_

2. _28_ , ___ , _32_ , ___ , ___ , ___ , ___ , ___ , ___

3. _40_ , ___ , ___ , _46_ , ___ , ___ , ___ , ___ , ___

Draw the hour hand on each clock to show the time.

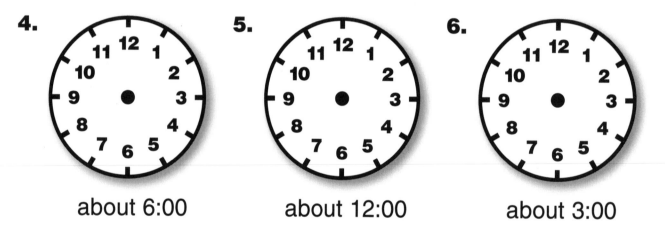

4.   **5.**   **6.**

about 6:00   about 12:00   about 3:00

Fill in the missing numbers. Count down.

7. _46_ , ___ , _44_ , ___ , ___ , ___ , ___ , ___ , ___

8. _23_ , ___ , _21_ , ___ , _19_ , ___ , ___ , ___ , ___ , ___

Use with or after Unit 3.

Practice Set 17

School Store

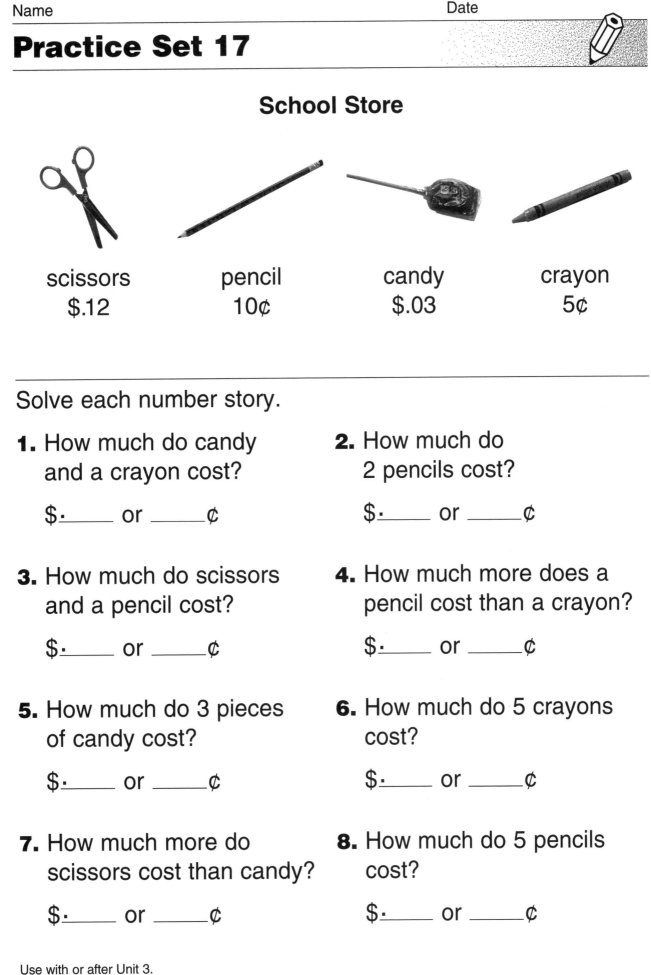

| scissors | pencil | candy | crayon |
| $.12 | 10¢ | $.03 | 5¢ |

Solve each number story.

1. How much do candy and a crayon cost?

$.___ or ____¢

2. How much do 2 pencils cost?

$.___ or ____¢

3. How much do scissors and a pencil cost?

$.___ or ____¢

4. How much more does a pencil cost than a crayon?

$.___ or ____¢

5. How much do 3 pieces of candy cost?

$.___ or ____¢

6. How much do 5 crayons cost?

$.___ or ____¢

7. How much more do scissors cost than candy?

$.___ or ____¢

8. How much do 5 pencils cost?

$.___ or ____¢

Use with or after Unit 3.

Practice Set 18

Write one more.

1. _19_ , _____   **2.** _32_ , _____   **3.** _50_ , _____

4. _37_ , _____   **5.** _23_ , _____   **6.** _49_ , _____

7. _13_ , _____   **8.** _44_ , _____   **9.** _30_ , _____

Write one less.

10. _____ , _12_   **11.** _____ , _19_   **12.** _____ , _30_

13. _____ , _25_   **14.** _____ , _37_   **15.** _____ , _45_

16. _____ , _39_   **17.** _____ , _16_   **18.** _____ , _41_

What's My Rule?

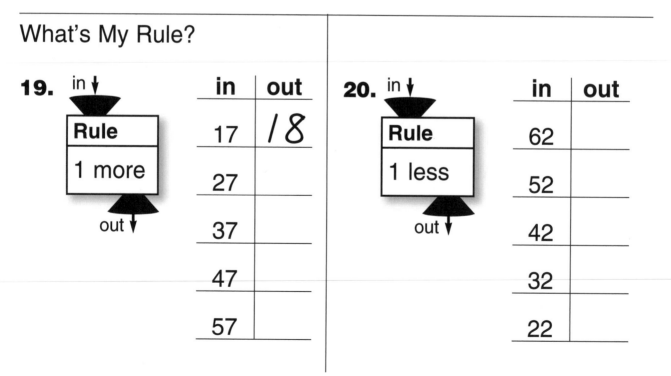

19.

in	out
17	18
27	
37	
47	
57	

Rule: 1 more

20.

in	out
62	
52	
42	
32	
22	

Rule: 1 less

Use with or after Unit 3.

Practice Set 19

Fill in the square under the time that
matches the clock face.

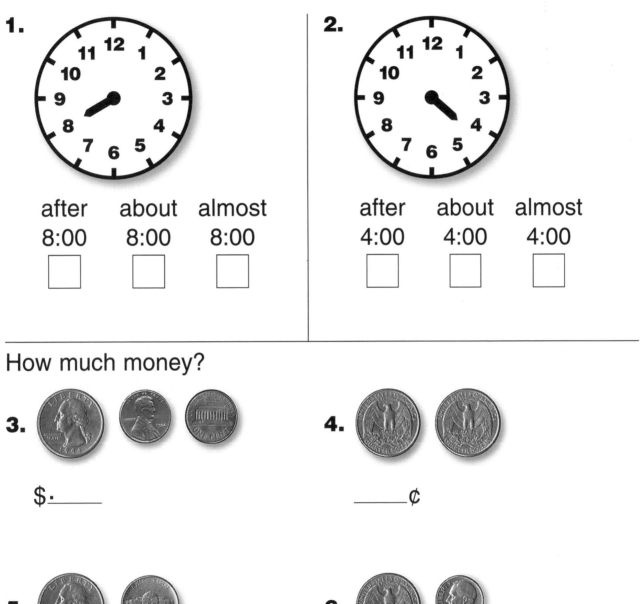

1.

after   about   almost
8:00   8:00   8:00
☐   ☐   ☐

2.

after   about   almost
4:00   4:00   4:00
☐   ☐   ☐

How much money?

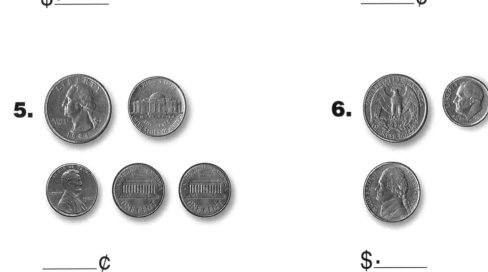

3.

$. _____

4.

_____ ¢

5.

_____ ¢

6.

$. _____

Use with or after Unit 3.

Practice Set 20

How many?

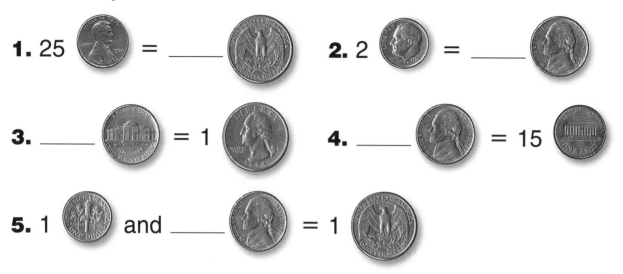

1. 25 (penny) = _____ (quarter)   **2.** 2 (dime) = _____ (nickel)

3. _____ (nickel) = 1 (quarter)   **4.** _____ (nickel) = 15 (penny)

5. 1 (dime) and _____ (nickel) = 1 (quarter)

Draw the hour hand on each clock to show the time.

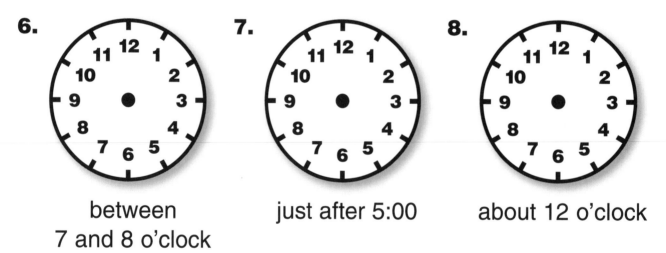

6.

between
7 and 8 o'clock

7.

just after 5:00

8.

about 12 o'clock

Fill in the unit box.
Write the missing numbers.

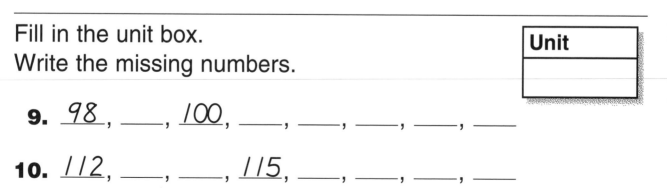

Unit

9. 98, _____, 100, _____, _____, _____, _____, _____

10. 112, _____, _____, 115, _____, _____, _____, _____

Practice Set 21

Show the total. Draw Ⓠ, Ⓓ, Ⓝ, and Ⓟ.

1. [ ]   Total

                                                 $.28 or 28¢

2. [ ]   Total

                                                 $.41 or 41¢

Show 35¢ two different ways.

3. [ ]

4. [ ]

Fill in the unit box.
Count by 5s.

Unit

5. _35_ , _____ , _____ , _50_ , _____ , _____ , _____

6. _70_ , _____ , _80_ , _____ , _____ , _____ , _100_

Use with or after Unit 3.

Practice Set 22

How many dots? Write *odd* or *even*.

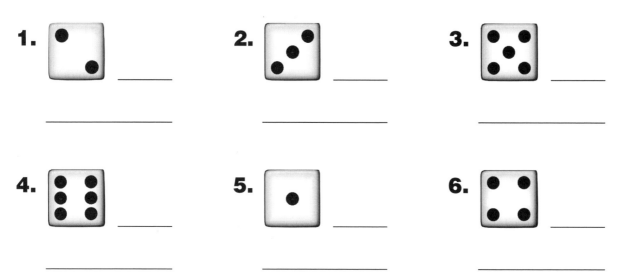

1. _____

_____

2. _____

_____

3. _____

_____

4. _____

_____

5. _____

_____

6. _____

_____

Count by 10s. Connect the dots.

7.

120
110
100
90
BEGIN
10
20
80
70   60
30
50
40

Practice Set 23

Count by 2s. Show your counts.

1.

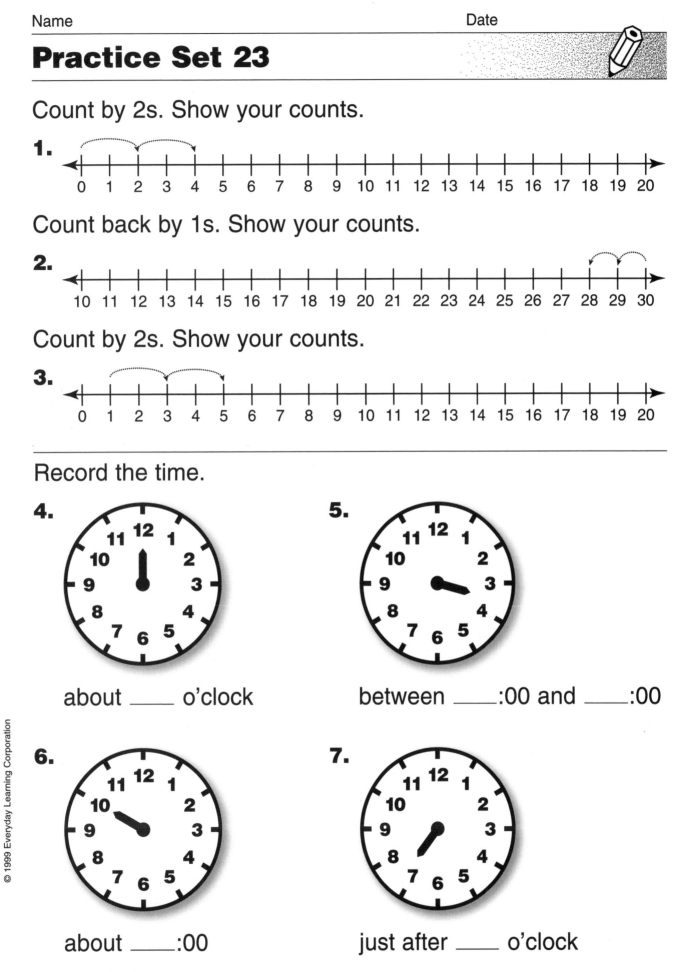

Count back by 1s. Show your counts.

2.

Count by 2s. Show your counts.

3.

Record the time.

4.

about _____ o'clock

5.

between _____:00 and _____:00

6.

about _____:00

7.

just after _____ o'clock

Use with or after Unit 4.

Practice Set 24

Write the missing numbers.

1.

-1 0 ___   ___   ___   ___   ___ 6

2.

8 ___ 10 ___   ___   ___   ___   ___

Fill in the frames.

Example:

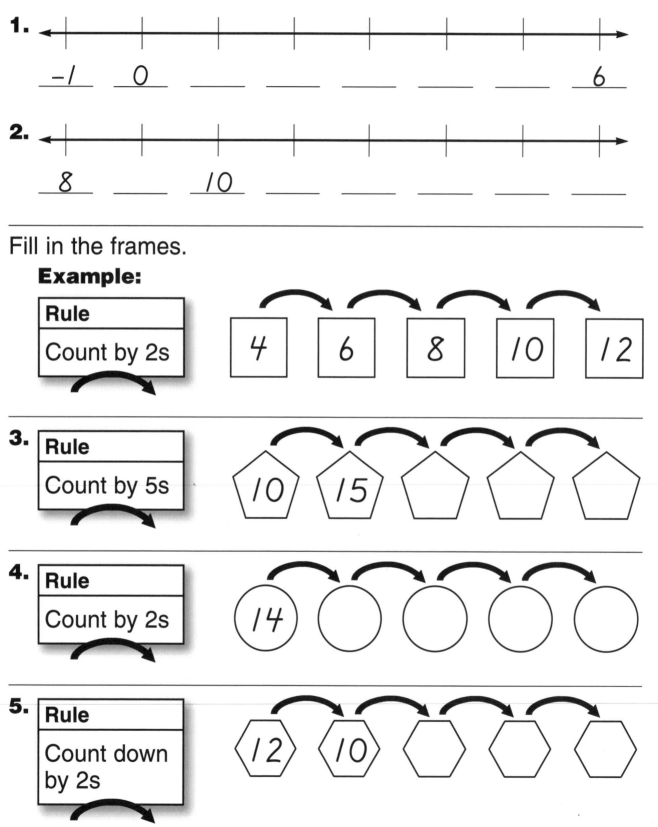

Rule
Count by 2s

4   6   8   10   12

3.

Rule
Count by 5s

10   15

4.

Rule
Count by 2s

14

5.

Rule
Count down by 2s

12   10

Practice Set 25

1. Count by 2s. Put an **X** over each correct number.

									0
1	~~2~~	3	~~4~~	5	~~6~~	7	8	9	10
11	12	13	14	15	16	17	18	19	20
21	22	23	24	25	26	27	28	29	30
31	32	33	34	35	36	37	38	39	40
41	42	43	44	45	46	47	48	49	50
51	52	53	54	55	56	57	58	59	60
61	62	63	64	65	66	67	68	69	70
71	72	73	74	75	76	77	78	79	80
81	82	83	84	85	86	87	88	89	90
91	92	93	94	95	96	97	98	99	100
101	102	103	104	105	106	107	108	109	110

Use the tally chart. Answer each question.

Favorite Animal

Horse	⊬⊬ ///
Elephant	///
Dog	⊬⊬ ⊬⊬ ⊬⊬ /
Monkey	⊬⊬ /
Cat	⊬⊬ ⊬⊬ //
Turtle	////

2. How many children chose a dog?

_____ children

3. Did more children choose a horse or a monkey?

_____

How many more?

_____ children

Use with or after Unit 4.

Practice Set 26

Write the numbers before and after.

1. _____ *19* _____   **2.** _____ *43* _____

3. _____ *30* _____   **4.** _____ *27* _____

Write 3 numbers for each domino.

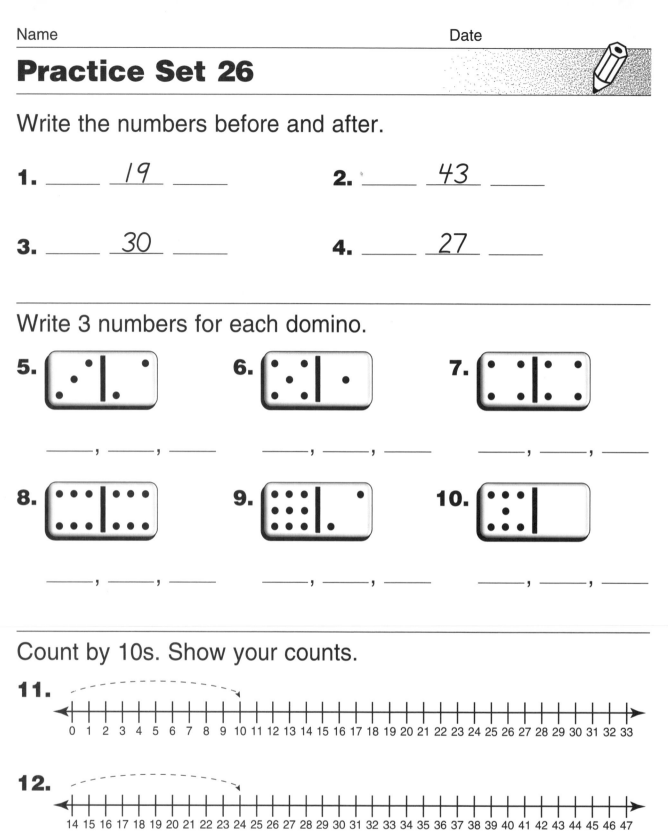

5.

_____ , _____ , _____

6.

_____ , _____ , _____

7.

_____ , _____ , _____

8.

_____ , _____ , _____

9.

_____ , _____ , _____

10.

_____ , _____ , _____

Count by 10s. Show your counts.

11.

0 1 2 3 4 5 6 7 8 9 10 11 12 13 14 15 16 17 18 19 20 21 22 23 24 25 26 27 28 29 30 31 32 33

12.

14 15 16 17 18 19 20 21 22 23 24 25 26 27 28 29 30 31 32 33 34 35 36 37 38 39 40 41 42 43 44 45 46 47

13.

26 27 28 29 30 31 32 33 34 35 36 37 38 39 40 41 42 43 44 45 46 47 48 49 50 51 52 53 54 55 56 57 58 59

Use with or after Unit 4.

Practice Set 27

How many?

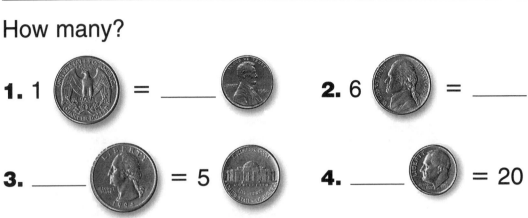

1. 1 (quarter) = _____ (penny)   **2.** 6 (nickel) = _____ (dime)

3. _____ (quarter) = 5 (nickel)   **4.** _____ (dime) = 20 (penny)

5. 15 (penny) = _____ (dime) and _____ (nickel)

Write the number that is 10 more.

6. _30_ , _____   **7.** _42_ , _____   **8.** _67_ , _____

Write the number that is 10 less.

9. _____ , _50_   **10.** _____ , _17_   **11.** _____ , _29_

Complete each number family.

12.

4 Family	
4	0

13.

5 Family	
2	3

Practice Set 28

Toy Store

ball
$.20

ring
12¢

crayons
$.25

bear
16¢

Solve each number story.

1. How much do
2 rings cost?

$·_____ or _____¢

2. How much do a bear
and a ball cost?

$·_____ or _____¢

3. Do crayons or a ball
cost more?

_____

How much more?

$·_____ or _____¢

4. How much do crayons
and a bear cost?

$·_____ or _____¢

5. Write a number story about
2 of the things at the toy
store.

Solve your story.

_____

_____

_____

_____

Use with or after Unit 4.

Practice Set 29

How many ☐s? Label *odd* or *even.*

1. 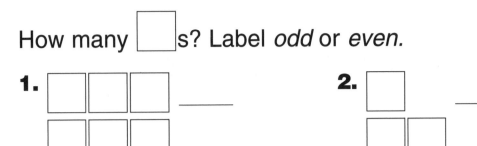 _____

_____

2. _____

_____

3. _____

_____

4. _____

_____

Count by 10s. Start at 6. Put an **X** over each correct number.

5.

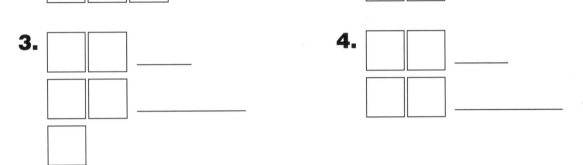

									0
1	2	3	4	5	X̶6̶	7	8	9	10
11	12	13	14	15	X̶16̶	17	18	19	20
21	22	23	24	25	26	27	28	29	30
31	32	33	34	35	36	37	38	39	40
41	42	43	44	45	46	47	48	49	50
51	52	53	54	55	56	57	58	59	60
61	62	63	64	65	66	67	68	69	70
71	72	73	74	75	76	77	78	79	80
81	82	83	84	85	86	87	88	89	90
91	92	93	94	95	96	97	98	99	100
101	102	103	104	105	106	107	108	109	110

Use with or after Unit 5.

Practice Set 30

What's My Rule?

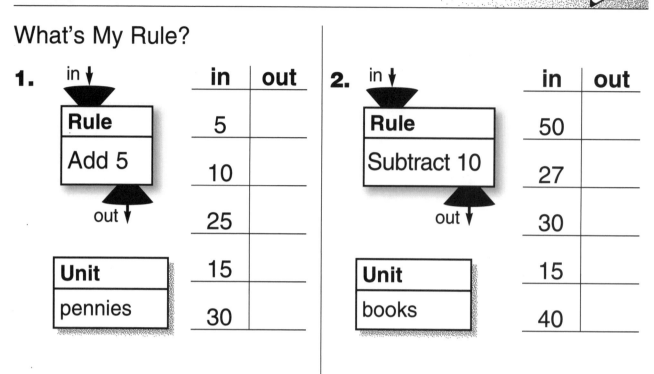

1.

Rule: Add 5

Unit: pennies

in	out
5	
10	
25	
15	
30	

2.

Rule: Subtract 10

Unit: books

in	out
50	
27	
30	
15	
40	

Fill in the five-minute marks on each clock.

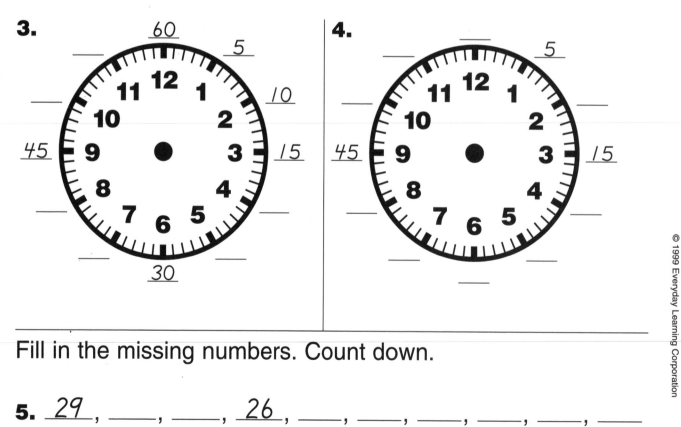

3.

4.

Fill in the missing numbers. Count down.

5. _29_ , ____ , ____ , _26_ , ____ , ____ , ____ , ____ , ____ , ____

Use with or after Unit 5.

Practice Set 31

Measure. Use inches.

1. |⎯⎯⎯⎯⎯⎯⎯⎯⎯⎯⎯⎯⎯⎯⎯⎯| = about ⎯⎯ inches

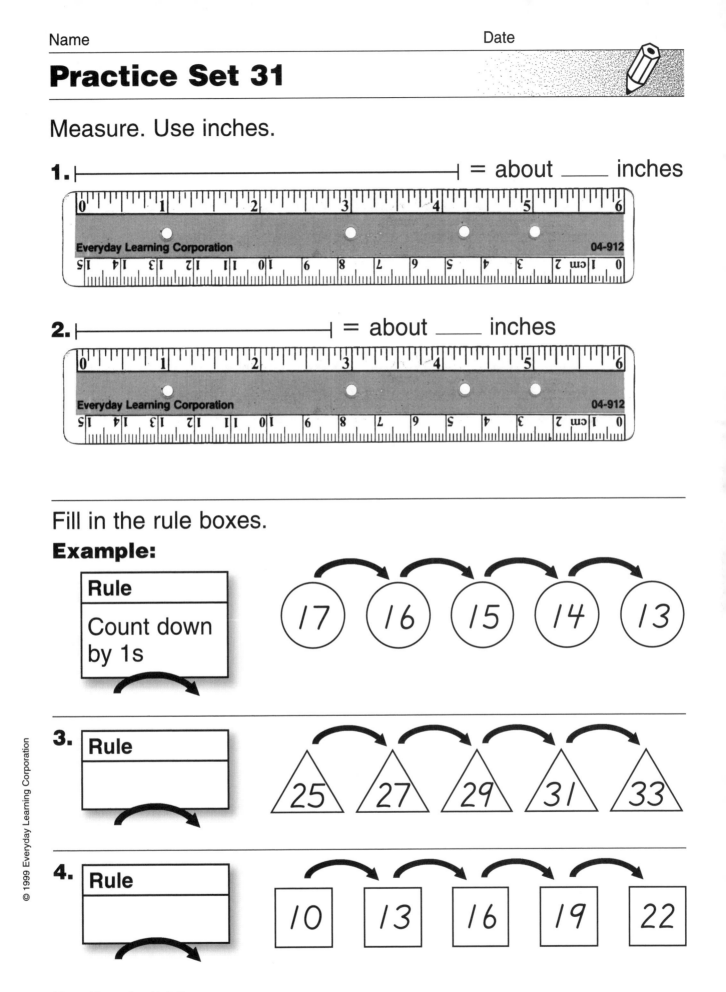

2. |⎯⎯⎯⎯⎯⎯⎯⎯⎯⎯⎯| = about ⎯⎯ inches

Fill in the rule boxes.

Example:

Rule
Count down by 1s

17   16   15   14   13

3.

Rule

25   27   29   31   33

4.

Rule

10   13   16   19   22

Use with or after Unit 5.

Practice Set 32

Count by 5s. Show your counts.

1.

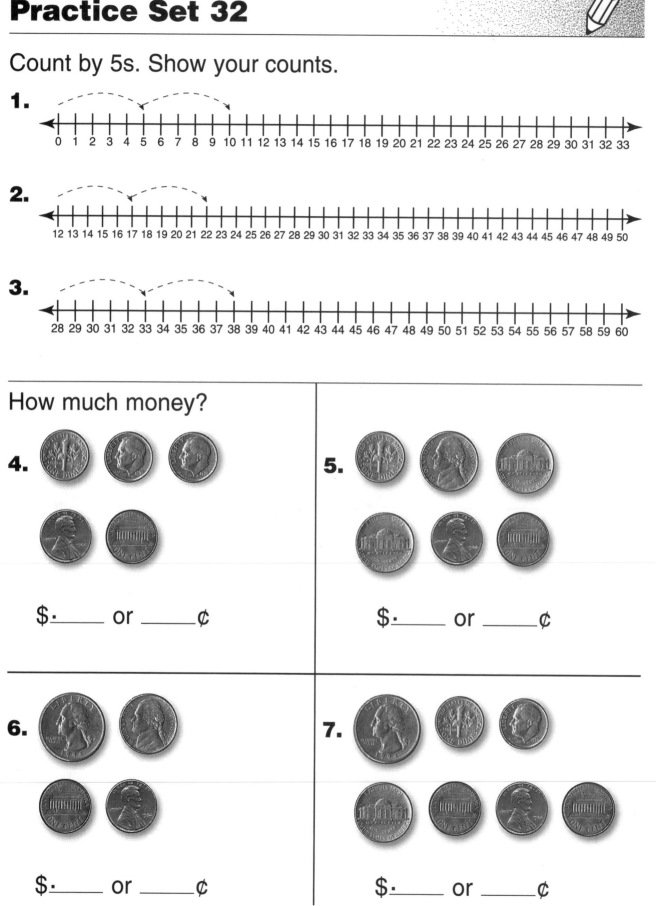

2.

3.

How much money?

4.

$·_____ or _____¢

5.

$·_____ or _____¢

6.

$·_____ or _____¢

7.

$·_____ or _____¢

Practice Set 33

Write the time shown.

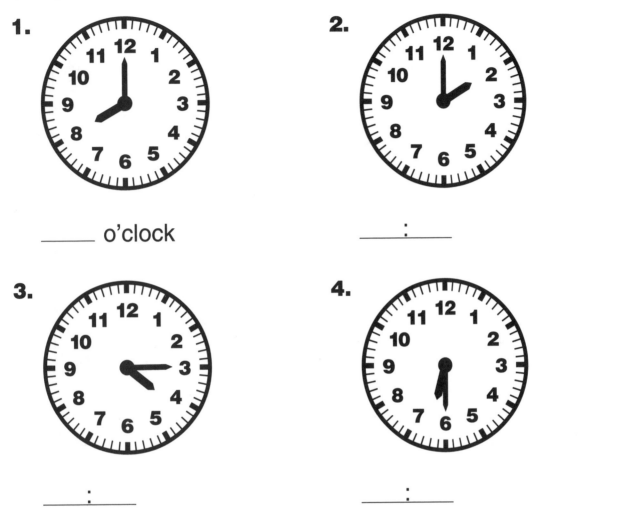

1.

_____ o'clock

2.

_____ : _____

3.

_____ : _____

4.

_____ : _____

Write 3 numbers for each domino.

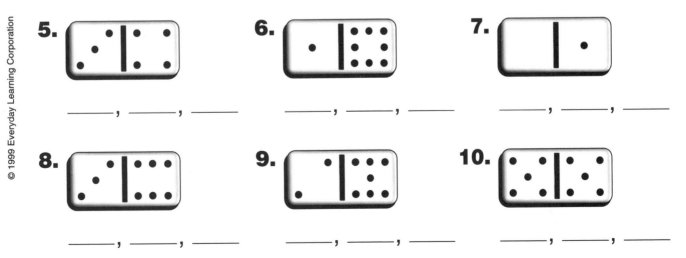

5. _____ , _____ , _____

6. _____ , _____ , _____

7. _____ , _____ , _____

8. _____ , _____ , _____

9. _____ , _____ , _____

10. _____ , _____ , _____

Use with or after Unit 5.

Practice Set 34

									0
1	✗2	3	4	5	6	✗7	8	9	10
11	✗12	13	14	15	16		18	19	20
21		23	24	25	26		28	29	30
31		33	34	35	36		38	39	40
41		43	44	45	46		48	49	50
									60
61	62	63		65				69	70
71	72		74	75	76	77	78	79	
81	82	83	84		86		88	89	90
	92	93	94	95				99	100
		103	104			107	108	109	
	112	113			116	117		119	120

1. Fill in the missing numbers on the grid.

2. Start at 7. Count by 5s. Put an **X** over the numbers.

3. Find three odd numbers. Draw circles around them.

Find the differences between the numbers.

4. 8 and 13 _____

5. 24 and 16 _____

6. 35 and 38 _____

7. 50 and 41 _____

Use with or after Unit 5.

Practice Set 35

Write the numbers before and after.

	before	number	after
Example:	49	50	51
1.		32	
2.	21		23

	before	number	after
3.		14	15
4.		60	
5.	39	40	

Measure. Use centimeters.

6.

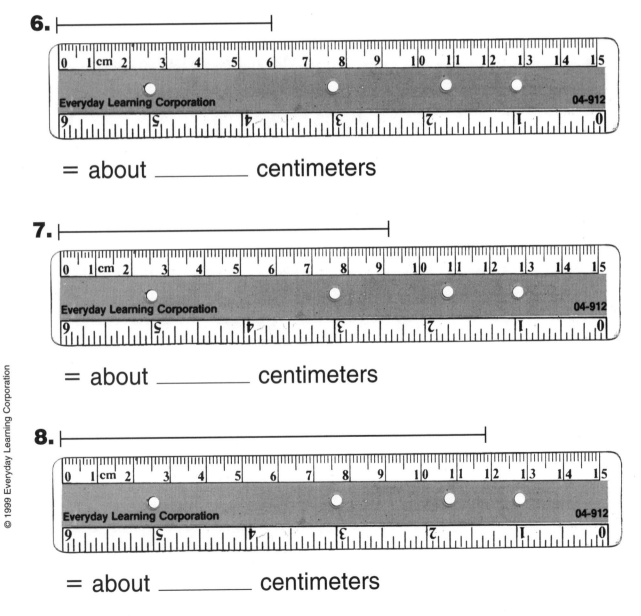

= about _____ centimeters

7.

= about _____ centimeters

8.

= about _____ centimeters

Use with or after Unit 5.

Practice Set 36

Use the tally chart. Answer each question.

First Grade Heights (inches)	
42	~~HHH~~
43	~~HHH~~ ~~HHH~~ ~~HHH~~ /
44	~~HHH~~ ~~HHH~~ /
45	~~HHH~~ //
46	////
47	//

How many children are

1. 44 inches tall?

_____ children

2. 46 inches tall?

_____ children

3. How many more children are 44 inches tall than 46 inches tall?

_____ children

Count by 10s.

4. _10_ , _____ , _30_ , _____ , _____ , _____ , _____ , _____ , _____

5. _14_ , _____ , _____ , _44_ , _____ , _____ , _____ , _____ , _____

6. _29_ , _____ , _____ , _59_ , _____ , _____ , _____ , _____ , _109_

7. _17_ , _____ , _____ , _____ , _57_ , _____ , _____ , _____ , _____

8. _8_ , _____ , _____ , _____ , _____ , _____ , _68_ , _____ , _____

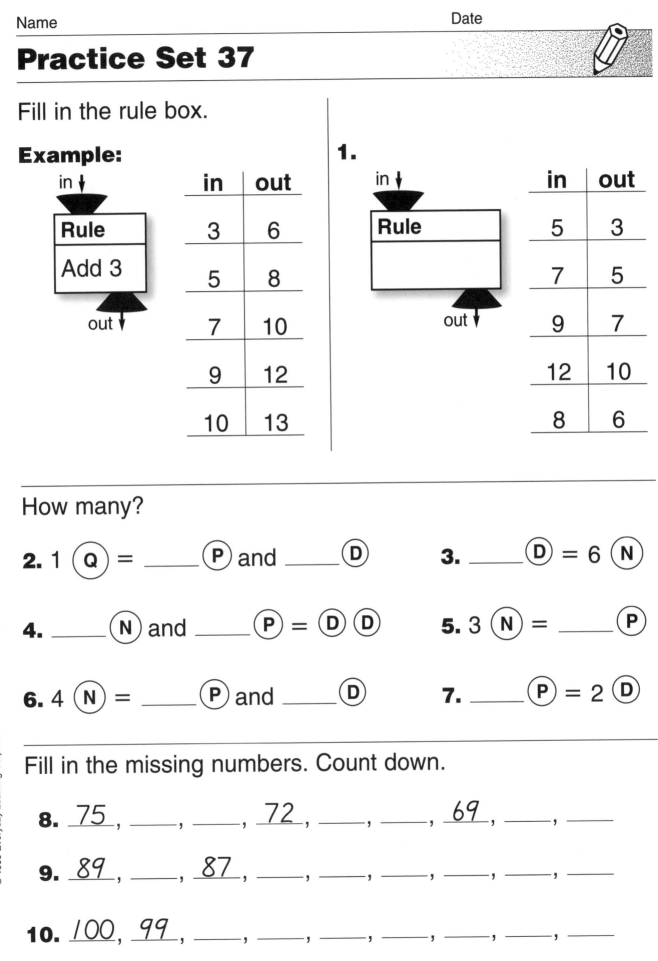

Practice Set 37

Fill in the rule box.

Example:

in ↓

Rule
Add 3

out ↓

in	out
3	6
5	8
7	10
9	12
10	13

1.

in ↓

Rule

out ↓

in	out
5	3
7	5
9	7
12	10
8	6

How many?

2. 1 (Q) = _____ (P) and _____ (D)

3. _____ (D) = 6 (N)

4. _____ (N) and _____ (P) = (D) (D)

5. 3 (N) = _____ (P)

6. 4 (N) = _____ (P) and _____ (D)

7. _____ (P) = 2 (D)

Fill in the missing numbers. Count down.

8. _75_ , ____ , ____ , _72_ , ____ , ____ , _69_ , ____ , ____

9. _89_ , ____ , _87_ , ____ , ____ , ____ , ____ , ____

10. _100_ , _99_ , ____ , ____ , ____ , ____ , ____ , ____ , ____

Use with or after Unit 6.

Practice Set 38

Write the time shown.

1.

_____ : _____

2.

_____ : _____

3.

_____ : _____

4.

_____ : _____

Fill in the missing numbers.

5. _100_, _____, _____, _103_, _____, _____, _____, _____, _108_

6. _127_, _____, _129_, _____, _____, _____, _____, _____, _____

7. _141_, _____, _____, _144_, _____, _____, _____, _____, _____

8. _168_, _____, _170_, _____, _____, _____, _____, _____, _____

Use with or after Unit 6.

Practice Set 39

Use <, >, or =.

1. 12 ☐ 19　　　　**2.** 43 ☐ 34

3. 115 ☐ 115　　　**4.** 58 ☐ 68

5. 124 ☐ 224　　　**6.** 300 ☐ 299

| < is less than |
| > is greater than |
| = is the same as |
| = is equal to |

| **Unit** |
| pounds |

Mark the end of the line segment for each length.

Example: 3 inches

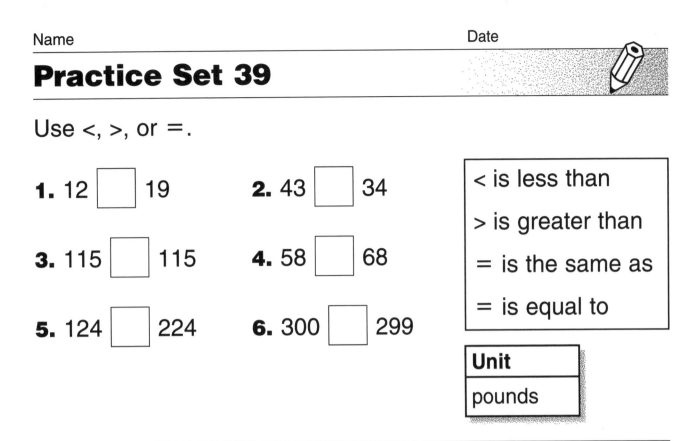

7. 5 inches

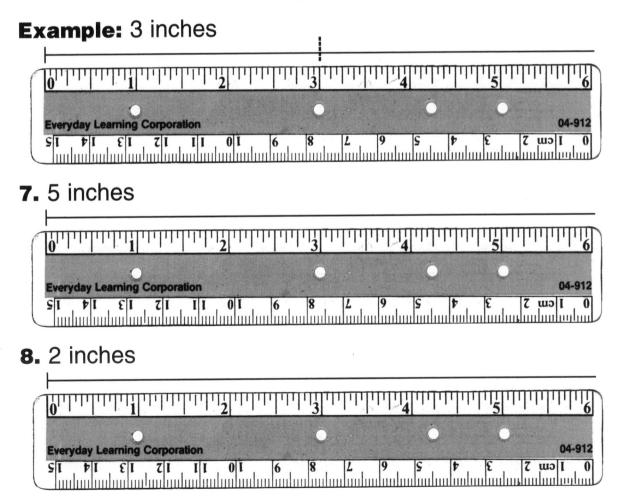

8. 2 inches

Practice Set 40

Use your calculator. Count by 2s.

Example: Press | C | | 2 | | + | | 2 | | =/R | | =/R | | =/R | | =/R |

1. _2_ , _4_ , _6_ , _8_ , ____ , ____ , ____ , ____ , ____

_20_ , ____ , ____ , ____ , ____ , ____ , ____ , ____ , ____

____ , ____ , ____ , ____ , ____ , ____ , ____ , ____ , _54_

Fill in the rule boxes. Complete the frames.

Example:

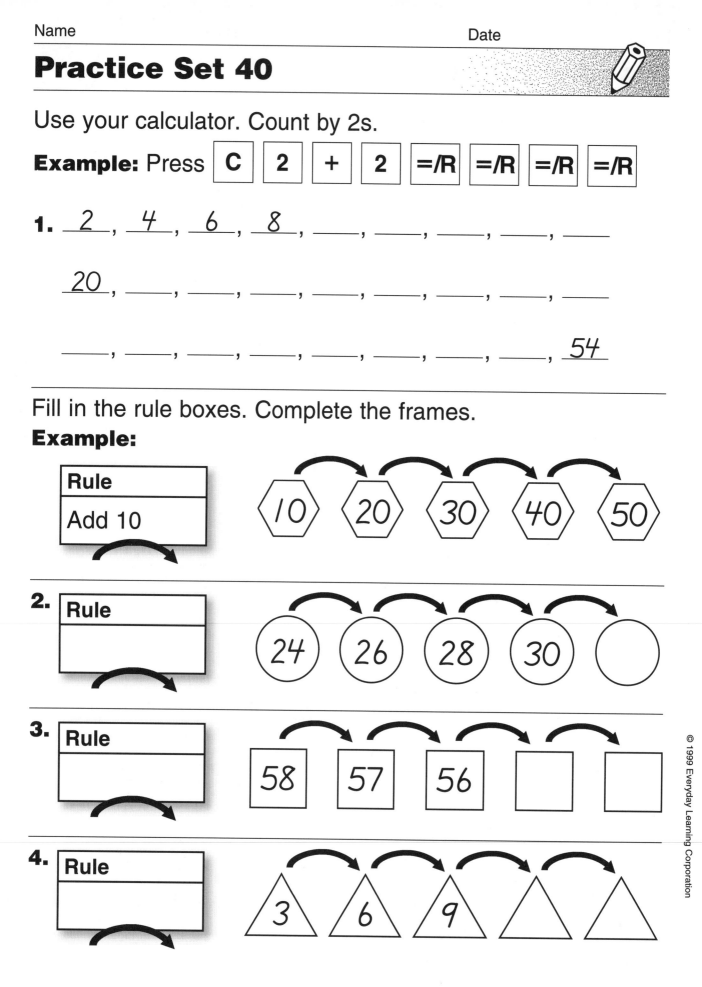

| **Rule** |
| Add 10 |

10   20   30   40   50

2. | **Rule** | |
| | |

24   26   28   30   ◯

3. | **Rule** | |
| | |

58   57   56   ▢   ▢

4. | **Rule** | |
| | |

3   6   9   △   △

Practice Set 41

Count by 5s. Start at 50.

Practice Set 42

Use < for less than; > for more than; = for equal.

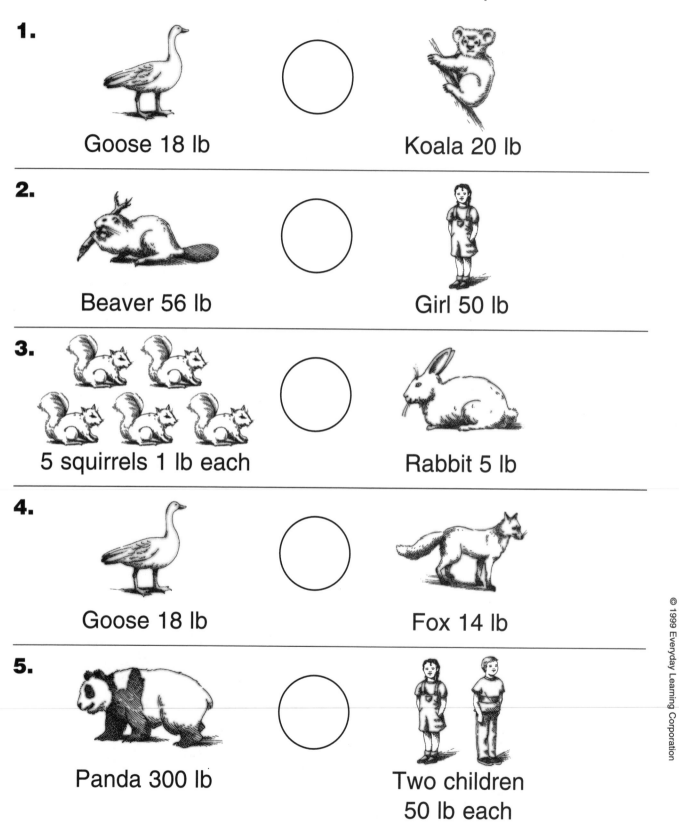

1.

Goose 18 lb ◯ Koala 20 lb

2.

Beaver 56 lb ◯ Girl 50 lb

3.

5 squirrels 1 lb each ◯ Rabbit 5 lb

4.

Goose 18 lb ◯ Fox 14 lb

5.

Panda 300 lb ◯ Two children
50 lb each

Use with or after Unit 6.

Practice Set 43

Show the total. Draw (Q), (D), (N), and (P).

1.

Total

$.27 or 27¢

2.

Total

$.22 or 22¢

3.

Total

$.46 or 46¢

Choose a total between 25¢ and 30¢.
Show your total.

4.

Total

_____¢

Fill in the missing numbers.

5.

24 , _____ , 26 , _____ , _____ , _____ , 30 , _____ , _____

Practice Set 44

Mark the end of the line segment for each length.

1. 8 centimeters

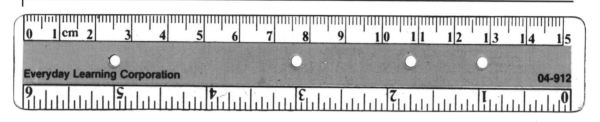

2. 14 centimeters

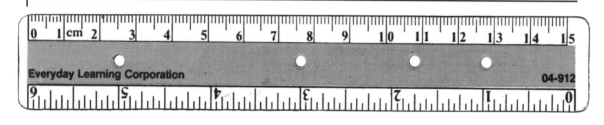

What's My Rule?

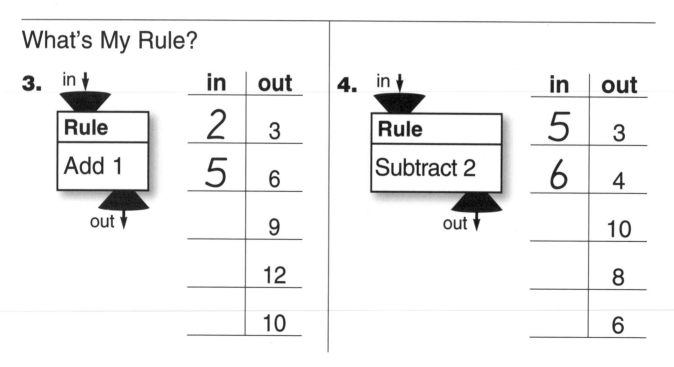

3.

Rule	
Add 1	

in	out
2	3
5	6
	9
	12
	10

4.

Rule	
Subtract 2	

in	out
5	3
6	4
	10
	8
	6

Practice Set 45

Write 5 names for the number.

Example:

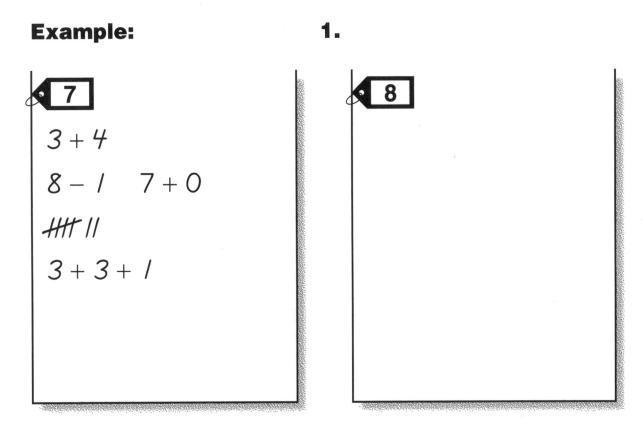

| 7 |

3 + 4

8 – 1   7 + 0

~~IIII~~ II

3 + 3 + 1

1.

| 8 |

Count by 10s.

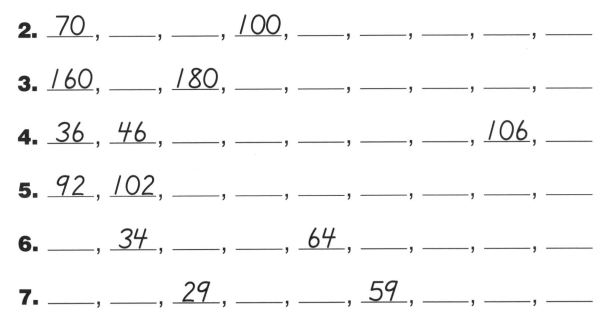

2. 70 , ___ , ___ , 100 , ___ , ___ , ___ , ___ , ___

3. 160 , ___ , 180 , ___ , ___ , ___ , ___ , ___ , ___

4. 36 , 46 , ___ , ___ , ___ , ___ , ___ , 106 , ___

5. 92 , 102 , ___ , ___ , ___ , ___ , ___ , ___ , ___

6. ___ , 34 , ___ , ___ , 64 , ___ , ___ , ___ , ___

7. ___ , ___ , 29 , ___ , ___ , 59 , ___ , ___ , ___

Use with or after Unit 7.

Practice Set 46

Match the clocks showing the same time.

Write 3 numbers for each domino.

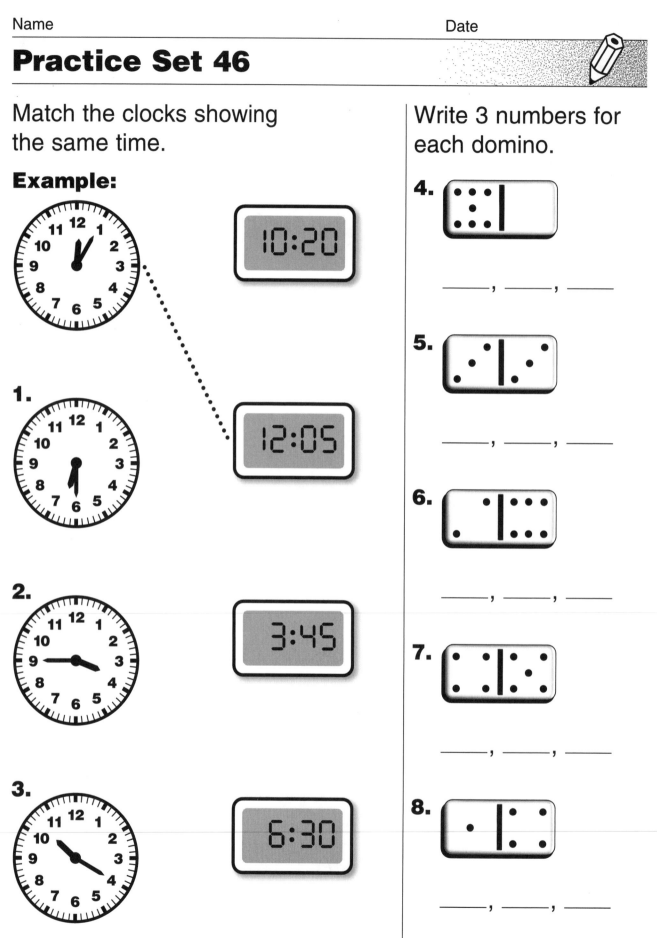

Example:

1.

2.

3.

10:20

12:05

3:45

6:30

4.

_____ , _____ , _____

5.

_____ , _____ , _____

6.

_____ , _____ , _____

7.

_____ , _____ , _____

8.

_____ , _____ , _____

Use with or after Unit 7.

Practice Set 47

Find the sums on the dice.

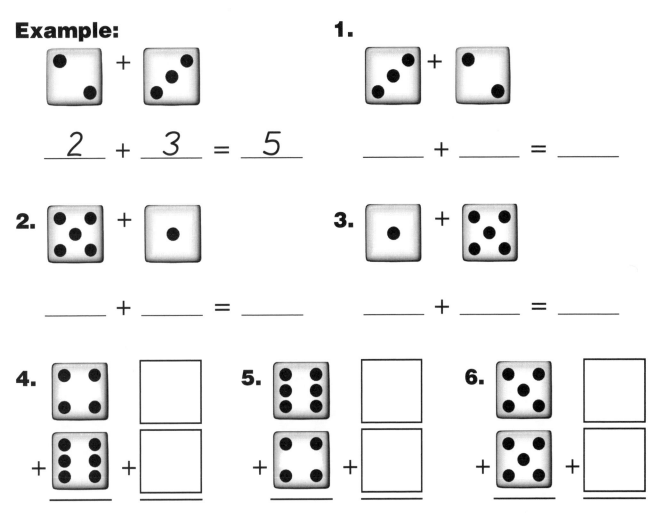

Example:

_2_ + _3_ = _5_

1.

___ + ___ = ___

2.

___ + ___ = ___

3.

___ + ___ = ___

4.

5.

6.

Fill in the unit box.

Fill in the missing numbers. Count by 5s.

Unit

7. _130_, _135_, _140_, ___, ___, ___, ___, ___, ___

8. _205_, ___, _215_, ___, ___, ___, ___, ___, _245_

9. _350_, _355_, ___, ___, ___, ___, ___, ___, ___

Use with or after Unit 7.

Practice Set 48

1. Complete the 2, 4, 6 family.

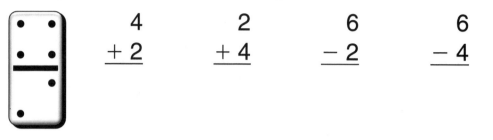

4	2	6	6
+ 2	+ 4	− 2	− 4

Domino Dots

2.

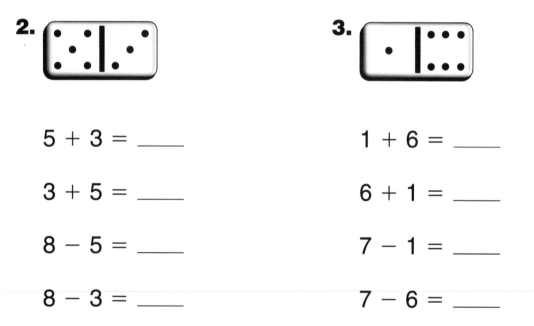

5 + 3 = ____

3 + 5 = ____

8 − 5 = ____

8 − 3 = ____

3.

1 + 6 = ____

6 + 1 = ____

7 − 1 = ____

7 − 6 = ____

Label each number as *even* or *odd*.

4. _____

5. _____

6. 14 _____

7. 100 _____

8. 39 _____

9. 77 _____

Use with or after Unit 7.

Practice Set 49

Write the fact family for the Fact Triangle below.

Example:

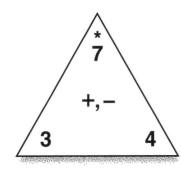

$7 = \underline{\quad 3 \quad} + \underline{\quad 4 \quad}$

$7 = \underline{\quad 4 \quad} + \underline{\quad 3 \quad}$

$7 - \underline{\quad 3 \quad} = \underline{\quad 4 \quad}$

$7 - \underline{\quad 4 \quad} = \underline{\quad 3 \quad}$

1.

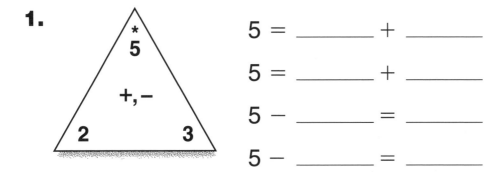

$5 = \underline{\qquad} + \underline{\qquad}$

$5 = \underline{\qquad} + \underline{\qquad}$

$5 - \underline{\qquad} = \underline{\qquad}$

$5 - \underline{\qquad} = \underline{\qquad}$

Use your calculator. Count by 5s.

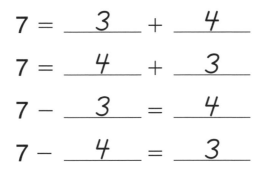

Example: Press | C | 5 | + | 5 | =/R | =/R | =/R | =/R |

2. $\underline{\quad 5 \quad}$, $\underline{\quad 10 \quad}$, $\underline{\quad 15 \quad}$, $\underline{\quad 20 \quad}$, $\underline{\quad 25 \quad}$, $\underline{\qquad}$, $\underline{\qquad}$, $\underline{\qquad}$, $\underline{\qquad}$,

$\underline{\qquad}$, $\underline{\qquad}$, $\underline{\qquad}$, $\underline{\qquad}$, $\underline{\qquad}$, $\underline{\qquad}$, $\underline{\qquad}$, $\underline{\qquad}$,

$\underline{\qquad}$, $\underline{\qquad}$, $\underline{\qquad}$, $\underline{\qquad}$, $\underline{\qquad}$, $\underline{\qquad}$, $\underline{\qquad}$, $\underline{\qquad}$,

Use with or after Unit 7.

Practice Set 50

1. Count by 3s. Put an **X** over each correct number.

2. Count by 2s. Circle each correct number.

									0
1	②	X	④	5	⑧	7	⑧	X	⑩
11	⑫	13	14	15	16	17	18	19	20
21	22	23	24	25	26	27	28	29	30
31	32	33	34	35	36	37	38	39	40
41	42	43	44	45	46	47	48	49	50
51	52	53	54	55	56	57	58	59	60
61	62	63	64	65	66	67	68	69	70
71	72	73	74	75	76	77	78	79	80
81	82	83	84	85	86	87	88	89	90
91	92	93	94	95	96	97	98	99	100
101	102	103	104	105	106	107	108	109	110

3. Write four numbers that you put an **X** over and circled.

_____   _____   _____   _____

4. Count by 6s. Color the squares with the correct numbers.

5. What do you notice about the squares you colored?

_____

_____

Practice Set 51

Make these true.

Example: $\boxed{14} < \boxed{20}$ **1.** $\boxed{18} > \boxed{}$

2. $\boxed{30} > \boxed{}$ **3.** $\boxed{} < \boxed{14}$

4. $\boxed{103} > \boxed{}$ **5.** $\boxed{9} = \boxed{} + \boxed{}$

What's My Rule?
Fill in the blanks.

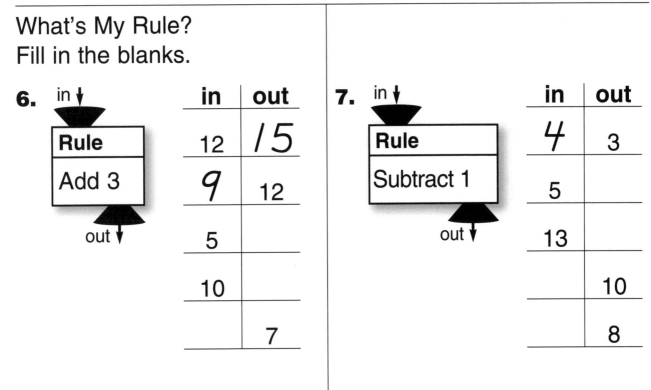

6. Rule: Add 3

in	out
12	15
9	12
5	
10	
	7

7. Rule: Subtract 1

in	out
4	3
5	
13	
	10
	8

Write the numbers before and after.

8. ____, _38_ , ____   **9.** ____, _92_ , ____

10. ____, _79_ , ____   **11.** ____, _100_ , ____

Use with or after Unit 7.

Practice Set 52

Fill in the missing numbers.

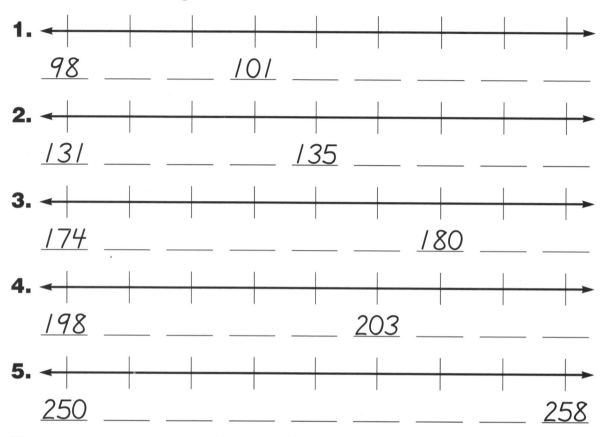

1. 98 ___ ___ 101 ___ ___ ___ ___ ___

2. 131 ___ ___ ___ 135 ___ ___

3. 174 ___ ___ ___ ___ ___ 180 ___

4. 198 ___ ___ ___ 203 ___ ___ ___

5. 250 ___ ___ ___ ___ ___ ___ ___ 258

Write 5 more names for each number.

6. **10**

$$5 \atop +5$$ $10 + 0$

7. **12**

$4 + 4 + 4$

Practice Set 53

Use the tally chart. Answer each question.

How Long We Can Stand on One Foot (seconds)

45	‖‖ /
50	‖‖ ‖‖ ///
55	‖‖ ‖‖ ‖‖ /
60	‖‖ ‖‖ ‖‖ ‖‖ ///
65	‖‖ ‖‖
70	‖‖ //
75	//

1. How many children could stand on one foot for 65 seconds or more?

_____ children

2. How many more children stood on one foot for 60 seconds than 55 seconds?

_____ children

3. How many children could stand on one foot for 50 seconds or less?

_____ children

4. How many more children stood on one foot for 65 seconds than 70 seconds?

_____ children

5. Write your own addition or subtraction problem using the tally chart.

_____

_____

_____

Practice Set 54

Write the turn-around facts for each Fact Triangle.

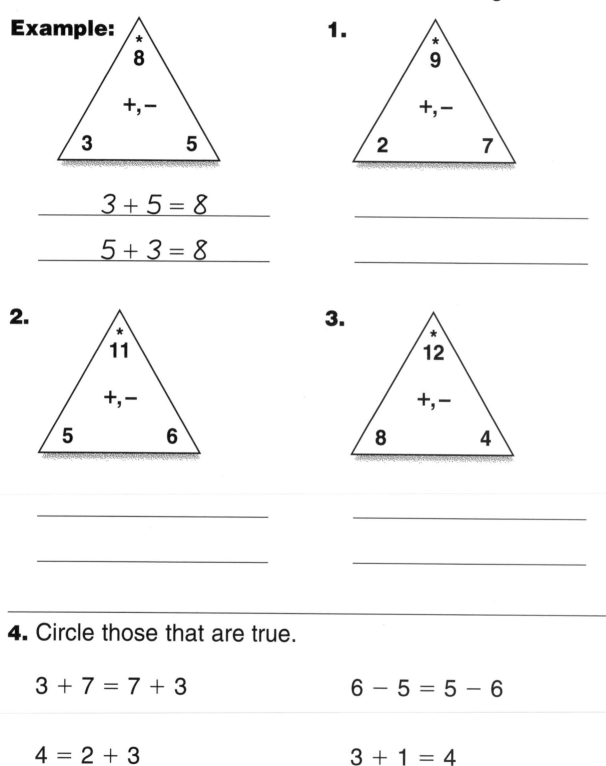

Example:

8
+,−
3   5

$$3 + 5 = 8$$

$$5 + 3 = 8$$

1.

9
+,−
2   7

_____

_____

2.

11
+,−
5   6

3.

12
+,−
8   4

_____   _____

_____   _____

4. Circle those that are true.

$$3 + 7 = 7 + 3$$ $$6 - 5 = 5 - 6$$

$$4 = 2 + 3$$ $$3 + 1 = 4$$

Use with or after Unit 8.

Practice Set 55

For each number, write the digit for each place value.

Example: 742

hundreds place __7__

tens place __4__

ones place __2__

1. 907

hundreds place _____

tens place _____

ones place _____

2. 186

hundreds place _____

tens place _____

ones place _____

3. 563

hundreds place _____

tens place _____

ones place _____

Addition Patterns	Subtraction Patterns
4. 3 + 0 = _____	**10.** 9 − 1 = _____
5. 4 + 0 = _____	**11.** 10 − 1 = _____
6. 5 + 0 = _____	**12.** 11 − 1 = _____
7. 6 + 0 = _____	**13.** 12 − 1 = _____
8. 7 + 0 = _____	**14.** 13 − 1 = _____
9. 8 + 0 = _____	**15.** 14 − 1 = _____

Use with or after Unit 8.

Practice Set 56

Fill in the frames.

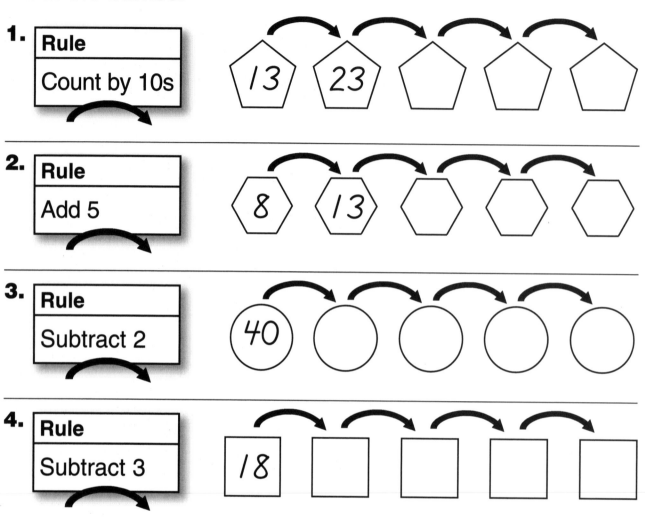

1. **Rule**
   Count by 10s

   13   23

2. **Rule**
   Add 5

   8   13

3. **Rule**
   Subtract 2

   40

4. **Rule**
   Subtract 3

   18

Write the number that is 10 more.

5. _64_ , ____   **6.** _39_ , ____   **7.** _41_ , ____

Write the number that is 10 less.

8. ____ , _99_   **9.** ____ , _27_   **10.** ____ , _53_

Use with or after Unit 8.

Practice Set 57

How much money?

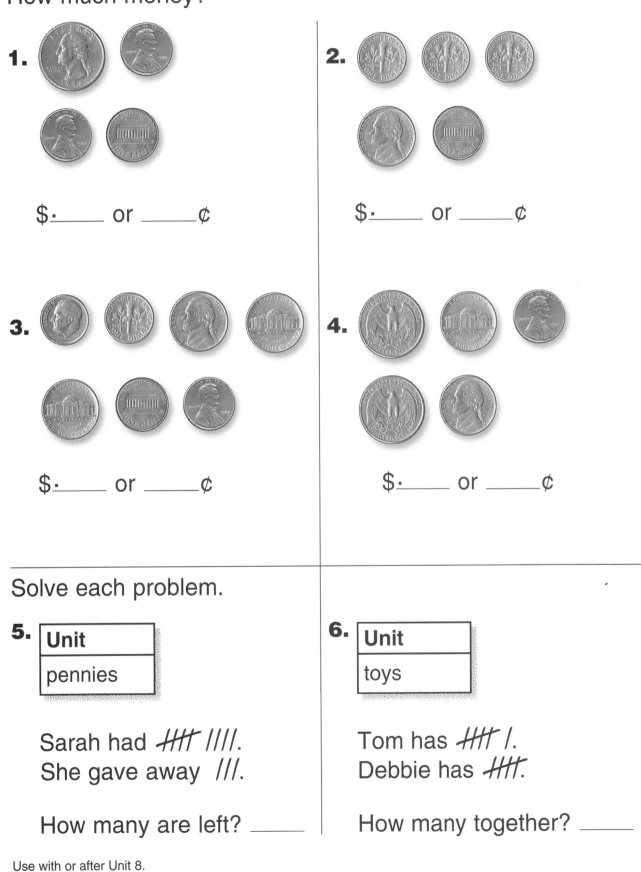

1. $.____ or ____ ¢

2. $.____ or ____ ¢

3. $.____ or ____ ¢

4. $.____ or ____ ¢

Solve each problem.

5.

Unit
pennies

Sarah had ~~HHH~~ ////.
She gave away ///.

How many are left? _____

6.

Unit
toys

Tom has ~~HHH~~ /.
Debbie has ~~HHH~~.

How many together? _____

Use with or after Unit 8.

Practice Set 58

List the fact family for each Fact Triangle.

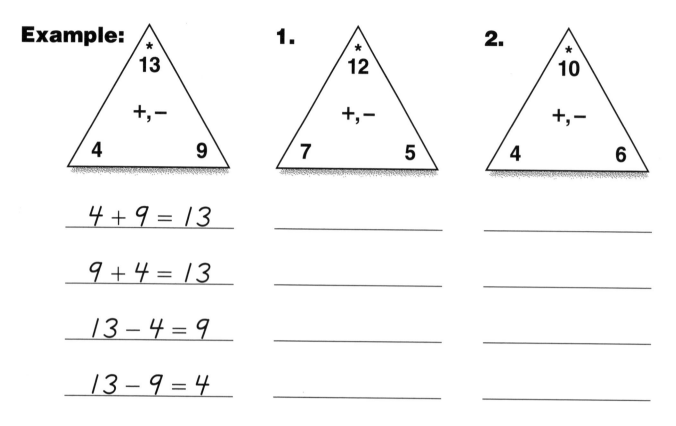

Example:

∗ 13

+,−

4　　9

4 + 9 = 13

9 + 4 = 13

13 − 4 = 9

13 − 9 = 4

1.

∗ 12

+,−

7　　5

_____

_____

_____

_____

2.

∗ 10

+,−

4　　6

_____

_____

_____

_____

Draw hands to show each time.

3.

8:25

4.

5:45

5.

12:10

Practice Set 59

Use <, >, or =.

<	is less than	
>	is greater than	
=	is equal to	

1. 2 dimes ☐ 15¢

2. 25¢ ☐ 6 nickels

3. 49¢ ☐ $.49

4. 13 pennies ☐ 2 nickels

5. 1 quarter, 1 dime, 2 pennies ☐ $.38

6. 52¢ ☐ 2 quarters, 2 pennies

Fill in the unit box. Find the sums.

Unit

7. 5
   + 3

8. 6
   + 4

9. 3
   + 2

10. 5
   + 0

11. 8
   + 5

12. 9
   + 1

13. 3
   + 6

14. 4
   + 7

15. 4
   + 2

16. _____ = 6 + 6

17. 3 + 9 = _____

Use with or after Unit 8.

Practice Set 60

Measure each object. Use inches.

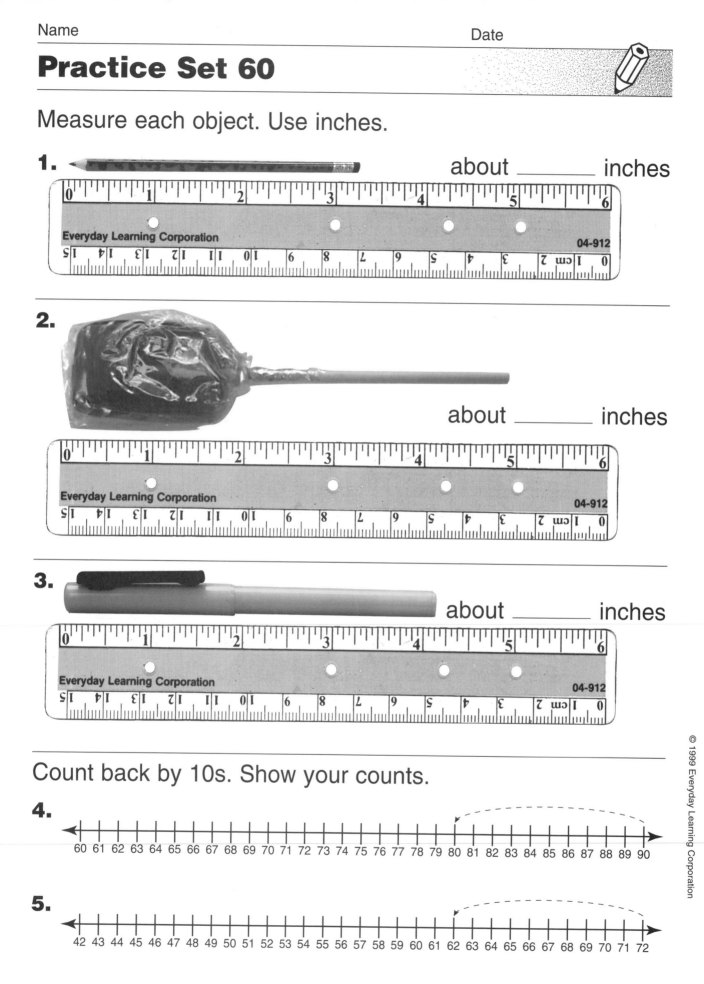

1. about _____ inches

2. about _____ inches

3. about _____ inches

Count back by 10s. Show your counts.

4.

60 61 62 63 64 65 66 67 68 69 70 71 72 73 74 75 76 77 78 79 80 81 82 83 84 85 86 87 88 89 90

5.

42 43 44 45 46 47 48 49 50 51 52 53 54 55 56 57 58 59 60 61 62 63 64 65 66 67 68 69 70 71 72

Use with or after Unit 8.

Practice Set 61

Write 3-digit numbers with:

Example:

4 in the hundreds place

7 in the tens place

2 in the ones place

_472_

1.

9 in the hundreds place

1 in the tens place

6 in the ones place

_____

2. 3 in the hundreds place

8 in the tens place

5 in the ones place

_____

3. 2 in the hundreds place

0 in the tens place

4 in the ones place

_____

Label each number as *even* or *odd.*

4. 12 _____   **5.** 29 _____   **6.** 95 _____

7. 100 _____   **8.** 126 _____   **9.** 201 _____

10. Write two even numbers between 250 and 300.

_____ , _____

11. Write two odd numbers between 100 and 150.

_____ , _____

Use with or after Unit 8.

Practice Set 62

Find each sum. Then color.

Colors: 6 yellow
          7 red
          8 green
          9 blue
       10 orange

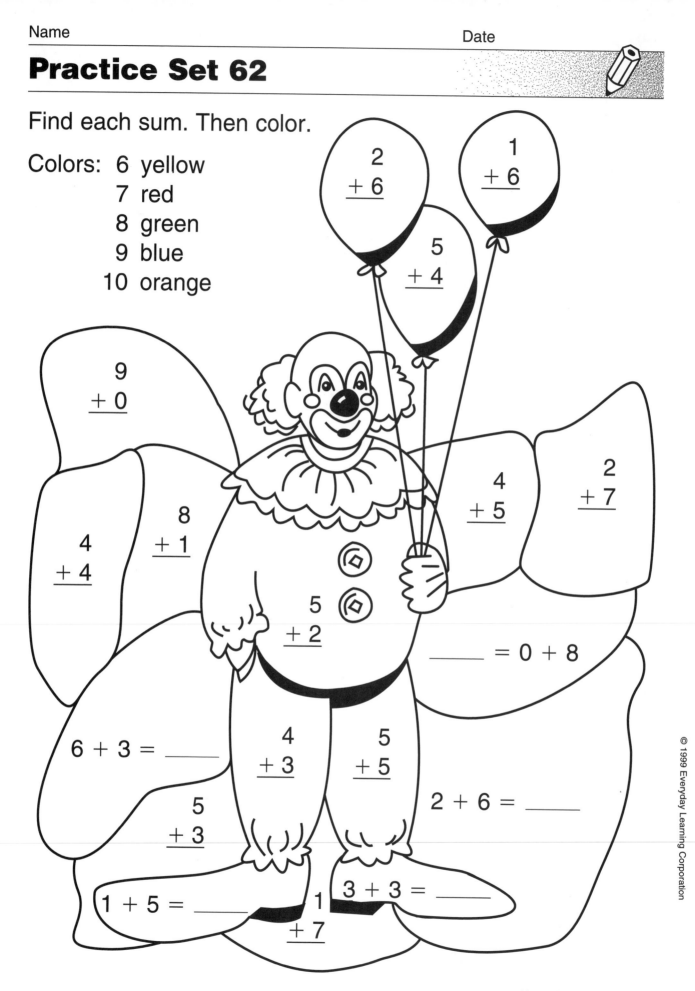

$2 + 6$

$1 + 6$

$5 + 4$

$9 + 0$

$4 + 5$

$2 + 7$

$4 + 4$

$8 + 1$

$5 + 2$

$\_\_\_ = 0 + 8$

$6 + 3 = \_\_\_$

$4 + 3$

$5 + 5$

$2 + 6 = \_\_\_$

$5 + 3$

$1 + 5 = \_\_\_$

$1 + 7$

$3 + 3 = \_\_\_$

Use with or after Unit 8.

Practice Set 63

Use your calculator. Count by 10s.

Example: Press | C | 1 | 0 | + | 1 | 0 | =/R | =/R | =/R |

1. _10_ , _20_ , _30_ , _40_ , ____ , ____ , ____ , ____ , ____ ,

____ , ____ , ____ , ____ , ____ , ____ , ____ , ____ , ____ ,

____ , ____ , ____ , ____ , ____ , ____ , ____ , ____ , ____

Write the following amounts of money.

Example: One dollar and sixty-two cents _$1.62_

2. three dollars and fourteen cents _____

3. two dollars and seven cents _____

4. one dollar and ninety-one cents _____

5. eighty-nine cents _____

Write the missing numbers.

6. ____ pennies = 1 dollar   **7.** 1 dollar = ____ dimes

8. 1 dollar = ____ quarters   **9.** 20 nickels = ____ dollar

10. 1 dollar = ____ quarters and ____ dimes

Practice Set 64

Fill in the rule boxes and the blanks.

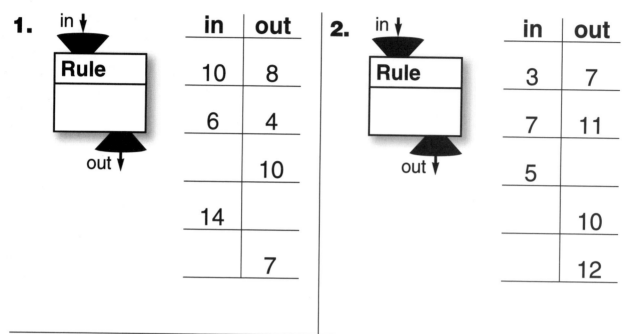

1.

in	out
10	8
6	4
	10
14	
	7

2.

in	out
3	7
7	11
5	
	10
	12

Cross out the names that do not belong.

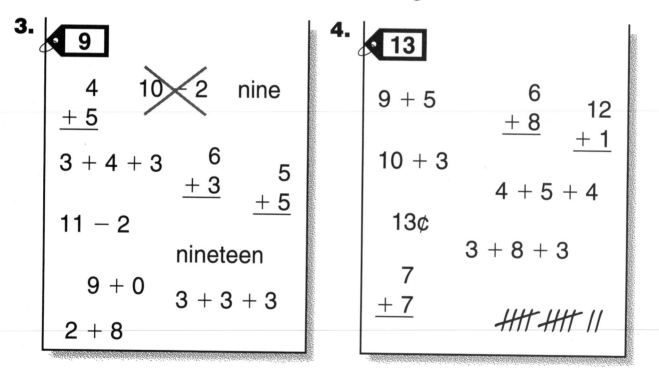

3. | 9 |

$\begin{array}{r} 4 \\ +5 \end{array}$ ~~10 − 2~~   nine

$3 + 4 + 3$ $\begin{array}{r} 6 \\ +3 \end{array}$ $\begin{array}{r} 5 \\ +5 \end{array}$

$11 − 2$

nineteen

$9 + 0$ $3 + 3 + 3$

$2 + 8$

4. | 13 |

$9 + 5$ $\begin{array}{r} 6 \\ +8 \end{array}$ $\begin{array}{r} 12 \\ +1 \end{array}$

$10 + 3$

$4 + 5 + 4$

$13¢$

$3 + 8 + 3$

$\begin{array}{r} 7 \\ +7 \end{array}$

|||| |||| ||

Use with or after Unit 9.

Practice Set 65

Draw the missing dots on the dominoes.
Write the missing numbers.

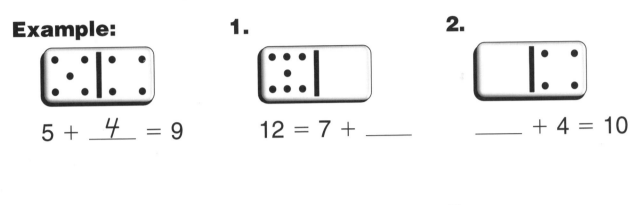

Example:

$5 + \underline{4} = 9$

1.

$12 = 7 + \underline{}$

2.

$\underline{} + 4 = 10$

3.

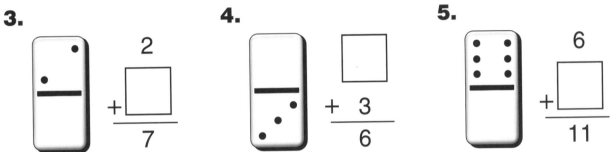

$\begin{array}{r} 2 \\ + \square \\ \hline 7 \end{array}$

4.

$\begin{array}{r} \square \\ + 3 \\ \hline 6 \end{array}$

5.

$\begin{array}{r} 6 \\ + \square \\ \hline 11 \end{array}$

6. Complete the grid.

231	232	233	234	235			238	239	240
241				245		247		249	
		253					258		260
261					266				
271		273	274			277			280
		283					288	289	
									300

Use with or after Unit 9.

Practice Set 66

Show the total. Draw (Q), (D), (N), and (P).

1.

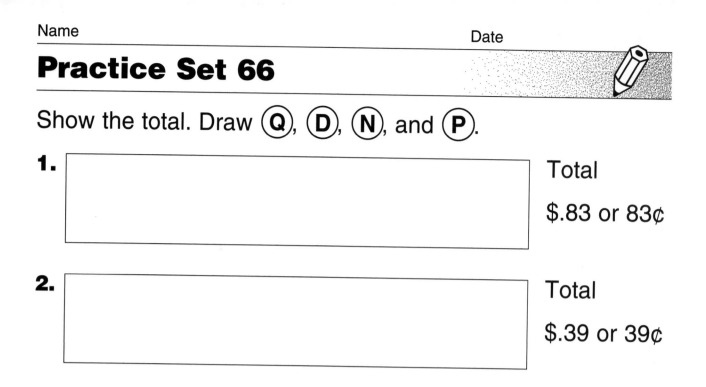

Total

$.83 or 83¢

2.

Total

$.39 or 39¢

Show each total using the fewest number of coins possible.

3.

Total

61¢

4.

Total

$1.07

5. Write the family of facts.

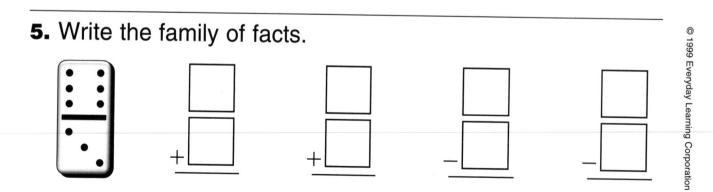

Name _____ Date _____

Practice Set 67

Animal Facts

Beaver
56 lb
30 in

Penguin
75 lb
36 in

Porpoise
98 lb
72 in

Koala
20 lb
24 in

Solve each problem.

1. Which is longer, the beaver or the penguin?

_____

How much longer?

_____ inches

2. Which weighs more, a beaver and a koala or a penguin?

_____

3. Which weighs more, 2 beavers or a porpoise?

_____

4. How much do a beaver and a koala weigh together?

_____ pounds

5. What is the total length of a porpoise and a koala?

_____ inches

6. How much longer is a penguin than a beaver?

_____ inches

© 1999 Everyday Learning Corporation

Use with or after Unit 9.

Practice Set 68

Write the missing number in each Fact Triangle.
Then write the turn-around facts.

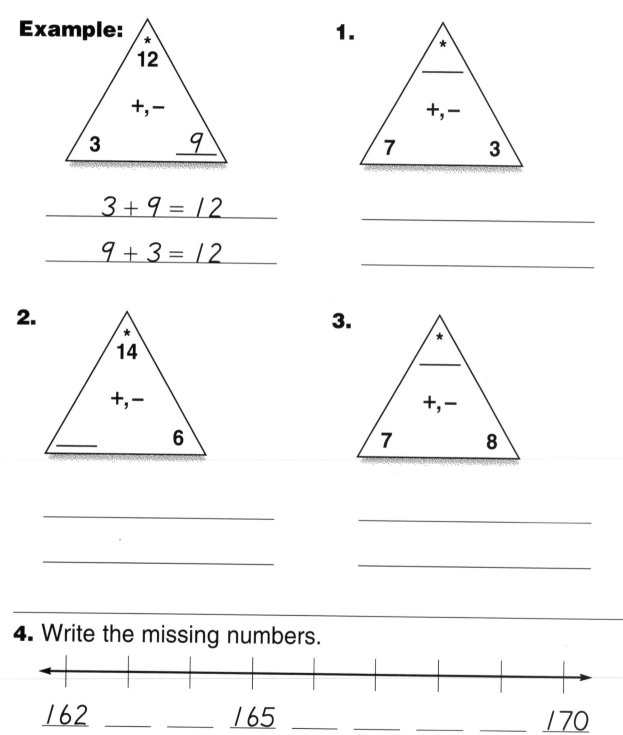

Example:

3 + 9 = 12

9 + 3 = 12

1.

2.

3.

4. Write the missing numbers.

162 ___ ___ 165 ___ ___ ___ ___ 170

Use with or after Unit 9.

Practice Set 69

Fill in the rule boxes. Complete the frames.

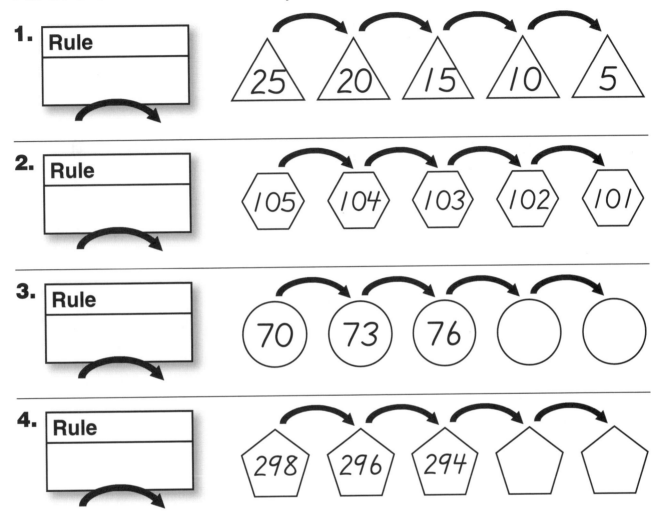

1. Rule _____

△ 25 → △ 20 → △ 15 → △ 10 → △ 5

2. Rule _____

⬡ 105 → ⬡ 104 → ⬡ 103 → ⬡ 102 → ⬡ 101

3. Rule _____

◯ 70 → ◯ 73 → ◯ 76 → ◯ → ◯

4. Rule _____

⬠ 298 → ⬠ 296 → ⬠ 294 → ⬠ → ⬠

Use the digits. Write the smallest and largest numbers.

Example: 2, 8, 5   smallest _258_   largest _852_

5. 7, 9, 3   smallest _____   largest _____

6. 9, 1, 4   smallest _____   largest _____

7. 6, 8, 5   smallest _____   largest _____

Use with or after Unit 9.

Practice Set 70

Measure each object. Use centimeters.

1.

= about _____ centimeters

2.

= about _____ centimeters

3.

= about _____ centimeters

Write each family of facts.

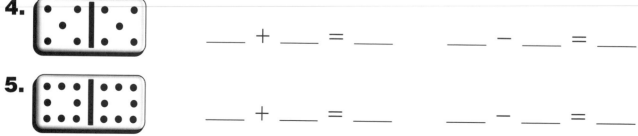

4. ____ + ____ = ____   ____ − ____ = ____

5. ____ + ____ = ____   ____ − ____ = ____

Use with or after Unit 9.

Practice Set 71

What time is it? Circle the correct time.

1.

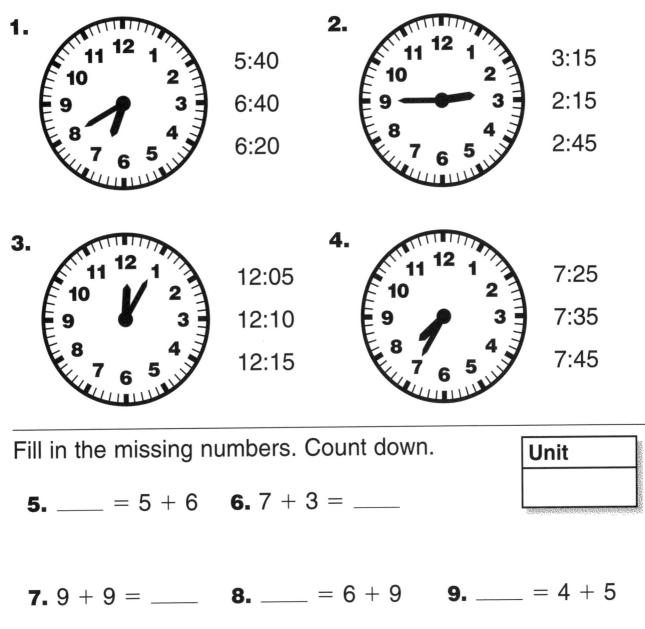

5:40

6:40

6:20

2.

3:15

2:15

2:45

3.

12:05

12:10

12:15

4.

7:25

7:35

7:45

Fill in the missing numbers. Count down.

Unit

5. ____ = 5 + 6   **6.** 7 + 3 = ____

7. 9 + 9 = ____   **8.** ____ = 6 + 9   **9.** ____ = 4 + 5

10.　 7
　　　 + 7
　　　 ─────

11.　 8
　　　 + 4
　　　 ─────

12.　 9
　　　 + 3
　　　 ─────

13.　 2
　　　 + 8
　　　 ─────

14.　 4
　　　 + 9
　　　 ─────

Use with or after Unit 9.

Practice Set 72

Fill in the unit box. Fill in the blanks.

Example: 215 = __2__ hundreds __1__ ten __5__ ones

1. 87 = ____ tens ____ ones

Unit

2. 394 = ____ hundreds ____ tens ____ ones

3. 762 = ____ hundreds ____ tens ____ ones

4. 985 = ____ hundreds ____ tens ____ ones

5. 439 = ____ hundreds ____ tens ____ ones

Mark the coins you need to buy each item.

6. 74¢

7. 49¢

8. 85¢

Use with or after Unit 10.

Practice Set 73

Write the fraction that is shaded.

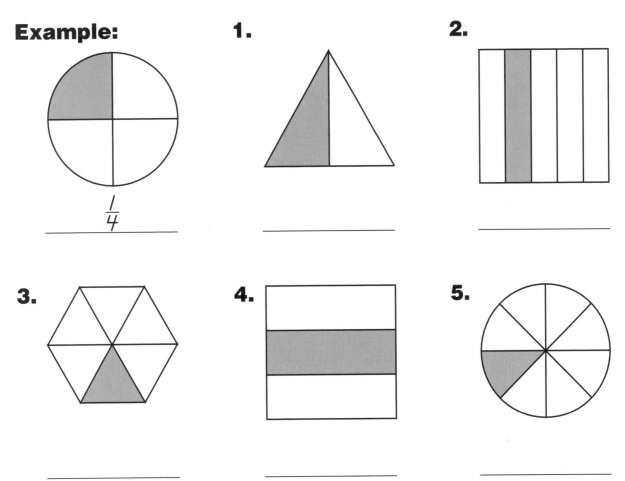

Example:

$\dfrac{1}{4}$

1.

_____

2.

_____

3.

_____

4.

_____

5.

_____

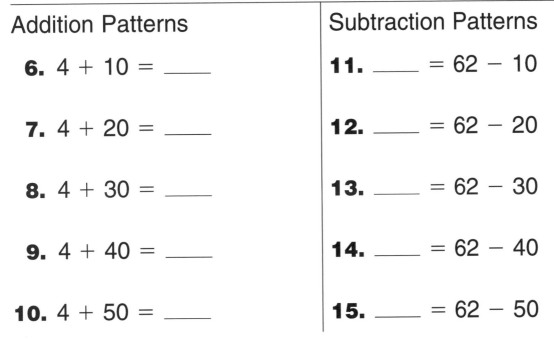

Addition Patterns	Subtraction Patterns
6. 4 + 10 = _____	**11.** _____ = 62 − 10
7. 4 + 20 = _____	**12.** _____ = 62 − 20
8. 4 + 30 = _____	**13.** _____ = 62 − 30
9. 4 + 40 = _____	**14.** _____ = 62 − 40
10. 4 + 50 = _____	**15.** _____ = 62 − 50

Use with or after Unit 10.

Practice Set 74

What's My Rule? Fill in the blanks.

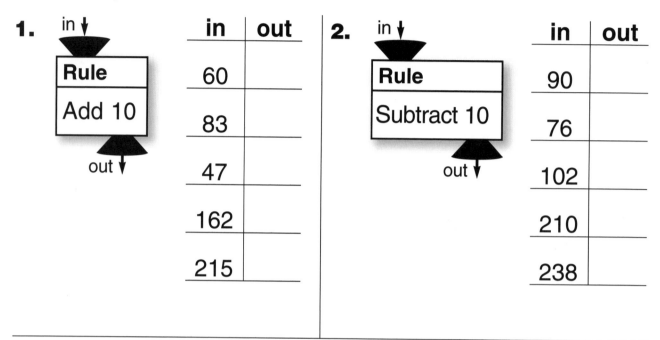

1.

in ↓

Rule
Add 10

out ↓

in	out
60	
83	
47	
162	
215	

2.

in ↓

Rule
Subtract 10

out ↓

in	out
90	
76	
102	
210	
238	

Write 5 more names for each number.

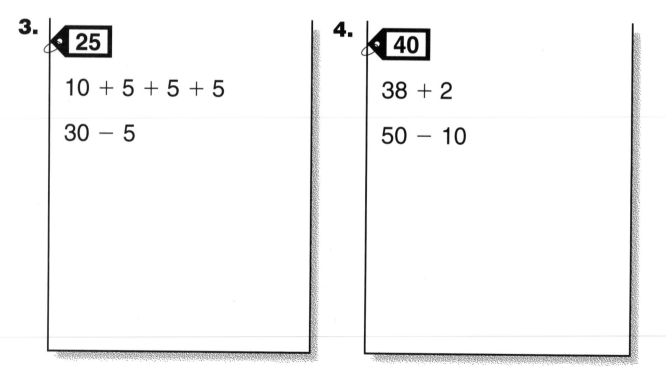

3.

25

$10 + 5 + 5 + 5$

$30 - 5$

4.

40

$38 + 2$

$50 - 10$

Practice Set 75

Write each number.

Example: four hundred fifteen _415_

1. ninety-two _____

2. sixty-seven _____

3. seven hundred eighty-three _____

4. two hundred seven _____

5. eight hundred thirty _____

Match.

6. two dollars and four cents $5.44

7. four dollars and twenty-four cents $2.40

8. three dollars and fourteen cents $4.24

9. two dollars and forty cents $2.04

10. five dollars and forty-four cents $3.14

Solve.

| < is less than |
| > is greater than |
| = is equal to |

11. _____ $+ 5 = 6 + 3$

12. $23 =$ _____ $+ 10$

13. $2 + 7 > 4 +$ _____

14. _____ $< 2 + 3 + 4$

15. $13 - 6 =$ _____ $- 2$

16. _____ $+ 2 = 8 -$ _____

Practice Set 76

Count by 10s. Fill in the missing numbers.

1. <u>50</u> , <u>60</u> , ____ , ____ , ____ , <u>100</u> , ____ , ____ , ____

2. <u>84</u> , <u>94</u> , ____ , ____ , <u>124</u> , ____ , ____ , ____ , ____

3. <u>127</u> , <u>137</u> , ____ , ____ , ____ , ____ , ____ , ____ , <u>207</u>

4. <u>225</u> , <u>235</u> , ____ , ____ , ____ , ____ , ____ , <u>295</u> , ____

Fill in the rule boxes. Complete the frames.

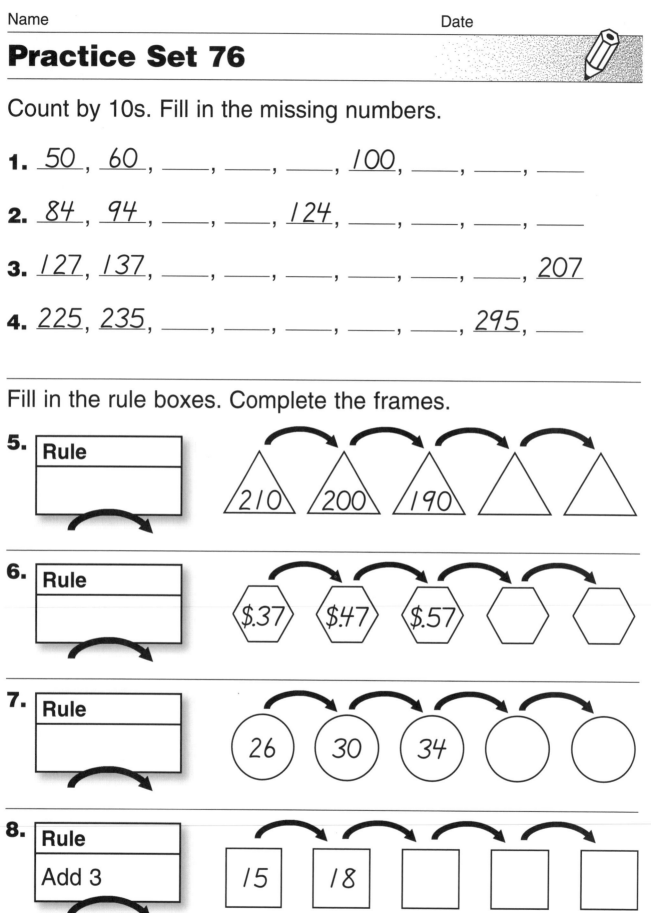

5. Rule

210 200 190

6. Rule

$.37 $.47 $.57

7. Rule

26 30 34

8. Rule
Add 3

15 18

Practice Set 77

Animal Facts

Trout	Woodpecker	Panda Bear	Fox
8 oz	2 oz	300 lb	14 lb
9 in	8 in	60 in	20 in

Solve each problem.

1. Which is shorter, the fox or the trout?

_____

How much shorter?

_____ inches

2. Which weighs less, the woodpecker or the trout?

_____

How much less?

_____ oz

3. What is the total length of the fox and the panda bear?

_____ in

4. Write your own problem about these animals. Solve your problem.

_____

_____

_____

Use with or after Unit 10.

Practice Set 78

Fill in the number-grid pieces.

Example:

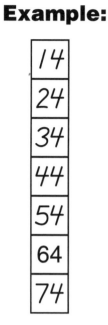

| 14 |
| 24 |
| 34 |
| 44 |
| 54 |
| 64 |
| 74 |

1.

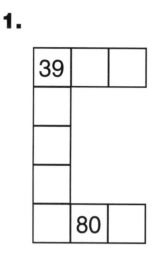

39

80

2.

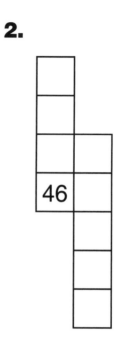

46

−9	−8	−7	−6	−5	−4	−3	−2	−1	0
1	2	3	4	5	6	7	8	9	10
11	12	13	14	15	16	17	18	19	20
21	22	23	24	25	26	27	28	29	30
31	32	33	34	35	36	37	38	39	40
41	42	43	44	45	46	47	48	49	50
51	52	53	54	55	56	57	58	59	60
61	62	63	64	65	66	67	68	69	70
71	72	73	74	75	76	77	78	79	80
81	82	83	84	85	86	87	88	89	90
91	92	93	94	95	96	97	98	99	100
101	102	103	104	105	106	107	108	109	110

3.

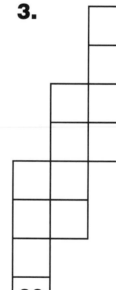

88

4.

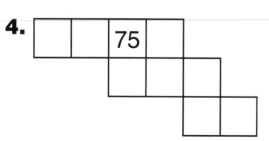

75

Use with or after Unit 10.

Practice Set 79

Use the digits. Write the largest and smallest numbers.

Digits	Smallest Number	Largest Number
3, 2, 7	**1.**	**2.**
5, 4, 8	**3.**	**4.**
2, 7, 9	**5.**	**6.**
6, 4, 6	**7.**	**8.**
1, 5, 3	**9.**	**10.**

Write the numbers in each Fact Triangle for the turn-around facts. Fill in the missing numbers.

11.

$+, -$

$$\underline{\qquad} + 5 = 7$$

$$7 = 5 + \underline{\qquad}$$

12.

$+, -$

$$\underline{\qquad} = 8 + 3$$

$$3 + 8 = \underline{\qquad}$$

13.

$+, -$

$$4 + \underline{\qquad} = 10$$

$$10 = \underline{\qquad} + 4$$

Use with or after Unit 10.

Practice Set 80

Museum Store

elephant	plane	dinosaur	magnet
72¢	$.27	59¢	$1.39

Solve each problem.

1. Which costs more, the elephant or the dinosaur?

_____

How much more?

_____ ¢

2. Which costs less, the dinosaur or the plane?

_____

How much less?

$. _____

3. Which costs more, 2 dinosaurs or a magnet?

_____

How much more?

_____ ¢

4. If you paid for an elephant with 3 quarters, how much change would you get?

_____ ¢

5. How much do 3 planes cost?

$. _____

6. If you paid for a magnet with $2.00, how much change would you get?

_____ ¢

© 1999 Everyday Learning Corporation